Steam in the Village

Steam in the Village

R A Whitehead

David & Charles

Newton Abbot · London · North Pomfret (Vt) · Vancouver

BY THE SAME AUTHOR

The Age of the Traction Engine
A Century of Steam Rolling
A Century of Service
Garretts of Leiston

UNIFORM WITH THIS BOOK

The Country Railway by David St John Thomas

ISBN 0 7153 7449 9
Library of Congress Catalog Card Number: 77-076101

Set in 11 on 13 point Times Roman
by Ronset Limited, Darwen, Lancs.
and printed in Great Britain
by Biddles Limited, Guildford, Surrey
for David & Charles (Publishers) Limited
Brunel House   Newton Abbot   Devon

Published in the United States of America
by David & Charles Inc
North Pomfret   Vermont 05053   USA

Published in Canada
by Douglas David & Charles Limited
1875 Welch Street North Vancouver   BC

Contents

All photographs in this book not otherwise acknowledged are from the author's collection

We have become diffident about our work and shy of professing interest for its own sake in what we do. Since we still spend about half our waking moments at work that attitude is our loss. The men of the steam days on the whole differed from us in this respect. They spent the greater part of their consciousness at work and were proud both of what they did and their ability to do it. *Jacket photograph (front):* The four Eddison and de Mattos men, posed in the late nineties beside the Fowler road locomotive in their charge, near Dorchester, knew there was no better maker and that the standard of their care of their gleaming charge was second to none. Noah Etheridge (in the stetson hat, *page 1*) was proud of his Garrett tractor and thresher at Blythburgh Hall (c 1910). Modest contentment at a job being done well stamps the driver and mate of Dunford & Sons' old Garrett wagon (*page 2*). Doing rough work (sand carting) and having only a year or two to run, the engine was, nevertheless, thoroughly clean, the brass gleamed, and though at full pressure and blowing off through the safety valves, it showed not one wisp of steam at any gland or joint. The woodland sawmillers' tractor (*page 3*) is seen here using its winding drum and a snatch block to haul a trolley load of logs up the tramline to the rack bench (*J. L. Middlemiss collection*). Charlie Joyce and his dog (*back cover top*) seen beside the Foster traction (owned by Eddison of Dorchester) with which he was baling hay in the 1914–18 War knew that all was as it should be – engine clean, brass bright and no leaks. (*Back cover bottom*) A woodland sawmill in Northumberland pre-1939 with a rack bench and a Marshall portable engine. Masters of improvisation the sawmillers have made everything, except the engine and bench, from what was to hand (*J. L. Middlemiss collection*).

Preface

I have always admired the preface which the late Frank Macey wrote to his admirable book *Specifications in Detail* in 1891. Consisting of two lines only it said 'This work is published in the hope that it may be found useful as a Reference Book for Architects'. I wish that I had so little to explain or excuse.

The idea of my writing a book upon the influence of the steam engine on the life of the countryside came from Mr David St John Thomas of David & Charles but I had been gathering material on what my friend Ronald Clark calls the 'folk-lore' of the traction engine for a long time before Mr Thomas suggested the form in which it might be published.

To all who have contributed to what follows and especially to those who have kindly allowed me to quote them direct I extend my sincerest thanks. A number of them, I regret to say, have died since the words quoted were written or spoken. The Road Locomotive Society, both officers and ordinary members, has done a great deal for the historian by seeking out and recording experiences and facts and often verifying them before they become erased by time, and I record my thanks to them as a body and in particular to three past presidents, namely the Reverend R. C. Stebbing, for reading the manuscript and supplying information, Ronald H. Clark for allowing me to draw upon his account of the Cringleford accident and Thomas B. Paisley for help and counsel with a great many matters.

The book is intended to help those who are interested in the life of the countryside, but who have never had anything to do with the part steam engines played in the complex structure of rural life, to gain an idea of the subject without becoming enmeshed in a dissertation upon either the economics or the technicalities of the steam engine. It is offered with diffidence and the hope that, in Frank Macey's words 'it will be found useful'.

R. A. Whitehead

Tonbridge,
Kent
20 October 1976

6

1. Prelude to Steam

Deep in a cleft in the North Downs not far from Meopham and only a short distance from Gravesend there was a water pumping station which delivered water to Gravesend. The engines in it were modern vertical triple expansions built by Markhams of Chesterfield, better known for their colliery winding engines. These engines epitomised in my eyes forty years ago and, in many ways, still do, in memory, though they have now given way to electric motors, the ultimate in steam power. Others were bigger, but none could have been better. The presiding genius for many years was an ex ship's engineer named Campbell – I never presumed to get on to Christian name terms with him – to whom the only acceptable standard was perfection. Not only was there never a suggestion of a knock or rattle or wisp of steam on the engines but the paintwork was a glistening vista of perfection, brass and copper – as a matter of course – were polished like mirrors and the bright plain steelwork was burnished as bright as plate. Even the handrails and standards of the walkways and steps were burnished and so bright were the steel

A scene in the Kentish fruit and hop country near Tonbridge in the closing years of the last century. The portable engine is pumping water for use in hop spraying

controls that I suspect that, like the levers in a railway signal cabin, they were chain burnished once or twice a day. A chain burnisher was a square, about 4 × 4in, of bright chain mail backed with a supple piece of leather. Gripped in the palm of the hand it was wrapped around the lever to be polished and worked briskly up and down. The application of the chain burnisher had the same effect on bright steelwork as boning upon the toe caps of a soldier's boots.

These same North Downs also harboured the picturesque complexities of the chalk quarry railways of the cement works situated in the Thames and Medway valleys, an intrusion of industry into an area, that, notwithstanding its otherwise deep rurality, was no more than thirty miles from London. Had the green belt not come into being there is little doubt that it would have been submerged under suburbia. As it happened, however, it survived and an interesting pocket of rural steam activity continued with it. Across it ran the railway from Swanley Junction to Gravesend West, a steam operated branch in an area otherwise wholly electrified. It would be pleasant to digress on the charms of the country railway but it is not really the province of this book and the subject has already been dealt with in its companion volume, David St John Thomas's *The Country Railway*.

The steam to be found on the roads and farms was fascinating enough by itself. A fair amount of corn was still grown into the twenties and thirties, enough to see several steam threshing contractors kept in work if not in affluence, notably Luke Terry & Sons of Malling, Thomas Wood & Sons at Crockenhill, Welban of Otford, Gates of Dartford, Nicholls at Rainham, Gibbs at Farnborough and the redoubtable John Young at Chelsfield. Like John Buchan, whom he admired, he was a Scot who had come south before 1914, finding opportunities too scarce in Scotland. Possessed of a droll poker-faced Scots humour and a lowland accent he once related to me in great detail the trouble he had had with the rim brake on his Marshall road engine which he attributed to shortcomings of design rather than workmanship and which he had discussed at length with the makers. 'Aye', he said, 'I knew their chief designer weel' – a long pause and a deep suck on his pipe – 'He was a Scotsman but o'course he couldna heelp thaat'.

Woods kept a set of Fowler steam tackle all through this period and it could, from time to time, be seen at work but they diversified as well into steam rolling and steam haulage. Terrys, too, undertook steam haulage but they also had a ragstone quarry which, as road work expanded in the twenties, eclipsed their other interests.

The other staple occupation of this absorbing area was paper-making – the big paper mill at Horton Kirby with its immense chimney and the smaller mill on the bank of the River Darenth at Eynsford – both steam powered. Brewing had declined and the only surviving independent brewery was Reffells at Bexley, right on the western edge close in to London, though just below the downs, at Westerham, there was the Black Eagle brewery where Messrs Bushell, Watkins & Smith made their delectable brew. Where the south end of the Darenth valley emerged from the downs there were two brickworks, Greatness and Dunton Green, both of

The steam wagon (Garrett No 33669) with which Cary & Grimsdell collected milk along the Piddle Valley, Dorset and which Victor Garrett encountered on his arrival in Dorchester

which possessed steam engines – the former having a large Robey single cylinder horizontal which is still at work. At Dunton Green works there was, at one time, a curious industrial locomotive, used to shunt skip wagons from the clay pit to the works which was, effectually, the boiler and engine of a traction engine mounted upon railway wheels.

The greatest treasure of them all, however, was the massive beam pumping engine used by the Sevenoaks Water Company only a stone's throw from Greatness. When it ceased work about 1934 it was over a hundred years old but, such was the lack of interest in old engines, it was slaughtered for the sake of the scrap and the engine house pushed over.

But even this array of engines was but a rump of what might have been found a decade earlier. When my friend Victor Garrett arrived in Dorchester to inspect the tottering Eddison Steam Rolling Co, deeply in debt and managed by an alcoholic, he would have arrived from London behind one of Drummond's elegant 4-4-0s and alighted almost under the shadow of the bulk of Eldridge Pope's brewery in which the yellow gault brickwork was interlaced with red brick quoins, arches and strings in the high Victorian manner and where every prime mover was steam driven. On that bright January morning in 1926 as he stepped out his mile long walk to Fordington there was little that was not steam driven – the flax mill, the flour mill (though it had help from a water wheel), Lott & Walne's foundry, the newspaper printing works, Cary & Grimsdell's creamery, the builder's saw bench

Marvin Lock's Foden wagon, newly rebuilt after an encounter with a Garrett owned by Samways of Weymouth. The rebuilding was done by Mr B. J. Fry whose flint-built engineering works at Fordington, Dorchester can be seen in the left background

and mortar pan – even the chaff cutter in Marvin Lock's stable. Marvin Lock also used an old Foden steam wagon (lately healed of the wounds received in a collision with another steam wagon owned by Samways of Weymouth) in his corn and coal merchants business, Cary & Grimsdell collected churned milk from the dairy farms along the Piddle valley with a pair of steam wagons, Doug Giffard and his father threshed by steam, John Groves & Sons and Devenish, the two Weymouth brewers, as well as the local firm of Eldridge Pope delivered their beer by steam, Jack Townsend, the local showman, had just bought his new Burrell road loco-motive 'Majestic', Ken Miles, at nearby Charminster, had newly gone over from steam tractors to a steam wagon built by Victor Garrett's own family firm of Richard Garrett & Sons Limited and, of course, everywhere there were the comings and goings of the Eddison fleet of steam rollers.

What he saw at the works at Fordington where Eddison owned and maintained nearly six hundred rollers, convinced him that the firm could be saved. It was to be the background of his life for the next twenty-one years, for as a result of his favourable report the creditors secured his appointment as managing director and he pulled the firm back from the brink of disaster. Eddisons were by far the largest employers in Fordington – B. J. Fry in his modest engineering works housed in a long low row of flint buildings almost opposite Eddison's yard employed only a handful of men and the mills employed a few more – but

Eddisons' men undoubtedly predominated. Fordington was probably the only village in England where the major male occupation was driving or maintaining steam rollers but in every village there was a pattern of a dominant industry – whether farming, quarrying, mining, fishing or manufacturing – and a secondary series of trades, providing the services which sustained the primary occupation. In larger villages, especially those furthest from a sizeable town, the non-conforming occupations might be numerous. There would, for instance, be a baker and his journeymen, a butcher, at least one boot repairer, a blacksmith and farrier, a grocer, probably several publicans or beer-house keepers, perhaps a miller, a candlemaker, a tailor, a saddler or even a brewer. Boot repairers were often boot-makers as well until the steady reduction in the cost of factory made boots in the second half of the last century priced village bootmakers out of the market. The skill was slow to die, however, and the products, carefully hand stitched with very strong waxed thread, heavily hobnailed and saturated in dubbin were, as a result of all these features – but mainly because of the strength and superiority of the stitching – very long lasting. In my own village, forty years ago, Dick Gardner, an old man even then, still had, and wore from time to time, a pair of heavy boots made for him by Jacob Playfoot, the village bootmaker, at the turn of the century.

The quiet agrarian revolution of the latter part of the eighteenth century which bore away the modified remains of the mediaeval system of land tenure with its common fields and multiplicity of small land-holders, created the means of feeding the large urban populations upon which the new industries of the country depended for workers. The old system had remained adequate whilst the total population was small and based upon the land. It had no surplus capacity, however, to support large town populations. Whilst no census was taken of population during the eighteenth century it is estimated that the rate of increase was very rapid and it had been suggested that between 1725 and 1800 the population may have increased four-fold.

Since farming as practised in the opening years of the eighteenth century did not produce sufficient surpluses to support a significantly larger population, the expansion of industrial towns in the second half of the eighteenth century created a market for food which the old methods of farming could not satisfy. Some foreign grain was attracted, particularly from France, but the demand also stimulated the owners of large estates into an improvement of the productivity and profitability of their lands and it was this promise of enhanced return from improved farms which provided the incentive to the progressive process of enclosures, the abolition of the small-holdings of the village cultivators – the 'three acres and a cow' men – and the incorporation of the land into the new improved farms thereby converting a high proportion of the rural poor from small-holders into landless wage earners. The process, under way by 1750, gained impetus as the growth of industrial towns pushed up demand and was further accelerated by the French Revolution, the rise of Napoleon and the state of conflict which lasted until 1814 by which time reliance on home produced cereals, was, more or less, total.

The cylinder cover of the 80in cylinder Cornish pumping engine at Robinson's shaft, South Crofty Mine, between Redruth and Camborne. The figure behind the cylinder is John Trounson. (*T. P. Roskrow*)

Improvement in farming methods was made possible by the work of such innovators as Jethro Tull (1674–1741), who devised workable forms of both the seed drill and horse hoe, and was led by progressive landowners of whom Coke of Holkham Hall, Norfolk is probably the most celebrated. The machines of the agricultural revolution were horse-drawn or hand-propelled. The horse often replaced human effort but it was not until well into the nineteenth century that steam supplemented on any serious scale the traditional agencies of the water wheel, the windmill, the horse or, to a lesser extent, the yoke of oxen in the service of agriculture.

The essentials of the agricultural revolution were the use of a proper rotation in cropping and manuring the land, the growing of roots for winter feeding of stock, better land utilisation and improved stock and plant strains. Harvesting crops and threshing out cereals remained manual tasks for some decades after the innovations had been accepted widely.

This is probably why steam came later to the farm than to other village occupations. Mining villages were already familiar with steam pumping of mines, though steam winding had lagged behind steam pumping. A large Boulton & Watt

How the portable engine was made self-moving by the addition of two chain sprockets, a pitch chain between them and a small man-stand at the rear. Steering was still by a horse in shafts at the front. The one in the picture was built in 1858 – the first made by Garretts who had begun building common portables ten years earlier.

beam pumping engine might have a cylinder as much as 90in in diameter, a cast iron beam weighing thirty-five tons and several hundred feet of iron or timber pump rodding extending down the shaft. Such an engine relied for its power not on the pressure of the steam from its boiler but upon the pressure of the atmosphere upon the top of the piston, the steam serving merely to displace air from the cylinder beneath the piston before being condensed to create the vacuum which allowed atmospheric pressure to do its work. An engine of the size outlined above might move $6\frac{1}{2}$ million gallons of water a day and yet be almost totally silent in its running. All that would be heard was the working of the valve rods, the motion of the beam through the air and the sound of the pump valves and rodding. The cylinder of such an engine was generally lubricated with a mixture of graphite and water but sometimes of tallow and graphite. Other moving parts would be oiled with melted lard or with vegetable oil. The cylinders of later engines in which steam under pressure, instead of merely the atmosphere, drove the piston were often lubricated by the fat cup, a noisome device consisting of a strong brass or gun-metal pot, with a screwed lid, connected by a pipe from its base to the steam space in the cylinder or having a threaded boss on the base screwed into a tapped

13

hole in the cylinder cover. Whilst steam was turned off the pot would be filled with waste suet or fat from the butcher and the lid replaced. As the engine worked steam entered the fat pot through the connecting pipe or through the drilled centre of the boss, cooking the suet and driving off the clarified fat from the greaves so that, by gravity, the fat ran back into the cylinder. The rancid odour which pervaded the whole fabric and engine house of an engine lubricated in this way had to be experienced to be believed.

Mining pumps and winders never wove themselves into the intimate fabric of the village life, however, for the reason that few except those paid to attend them came into contact with them. Colliers and surface men had, on the whole, enough to do with their own arduous duties without taking any interest in the steam engines whilst, except for small boys who might deliver snap to fathers or uncles in the engine house, other villagers scarcely saw them. Even the enginemen themselves held apart from their collier neighbours, being paid more and expecting to be respected accordingly. More than this, colliers knew that their very lives depended upon the care and integrity of the enginemen, particularly after the introduction of steam winding. A cage over-wound was hurled against the pit head gear, usually with the result that the winding rope broke and the cage crashed to the bottom of the shaft with fatal results to the passengers. Winding enginemen were expected to be abstemious or, better, teetotal, and regular chapelgoers were in great favour, a tradition that has obtained into our own day. All this helped to impart an esoteric and sacrosanct air to the enginemen of coal mines and to the engines themselves.

In the tin and copper mines of Cornwall, however, the cloak of detachment and mystery was less pronounced. The Cornish mines, unlike the northern coal mines which were owned, by and large, by the aristocracy or the very rich, singly or in alliances, were controlled by partnerships of adventurers of much humbler origins. Though coming from middle or working class backgrounds may not have made them less ruthless than the noble owners of the coal mines, they were nevertheless more readily seen as a part of the village community. It was Cornish engineers who chafed under the monopoly of steam pumps which Boulton & Watt enjoyed by virtue of their patent of the condensing steam engine. Cornish engineers pioneered the superior economy achieved by using the condenser in conjunction with steam above atmospheric pressure. Fuel economy was of little consequence at a colliery where the boilers were fired on smalls and other coals likely otherwise to have been wasted or sold at derisory prices. In Cornwall, where every ton had to be bought and bore heavy shipping and cartage costs, the saving of fuel was a pressing matter.

It was Richard Trevithick (1771–1833), one of the Cornish engineers locked in battle with Boulton & Watt over the latter firm's strangling patent of the condenser and the improvement of Cornish engines, who took the steps needed to bring steam engines out of the monastic seclusion of their engine houses – already, in any case, more part of the community life in Cornwall than elsewhere – and into

Aveling had very limited works facilities in the early 1860s and licensed the building of his designs of traction engine to other makers. This is an engraving of his second design of traction engine taken from a catalogue of Richard Garrett & Sons of Leiston

everyday life of the village. Steam engine development in Cornwall after the expiration, in June 1800, of Boulton & Watt's patent for the separate condenser became a separate and vigorous industry and Trevithick one of its most inventive practitioners. In 1800 and 1801 he built, jointly with his cousin Andrew Vivian, a self propelled steam road carriage which he followed, in 1804, by his celebrated steam locomotive for the Penydaren tramroad in South Wales, the first working steam railway locomotive. These engines dispensed altogether with the condenser and worked by the unassisted action of high pressure steam.

The strange instability in Trevithick's character which denied him most of the material benefits with which his inventive genius would otherwise have endowed him was allied at times to an astonishing clarity of vision, perhaps most remarkably displayed when he wrote 'Railways are useful for speed and for the sake of safety but not otherwise; every purpose would be answered by steam on common roads, which can be applied to every purpose a horse can effect'.

By this time he had a considerable practice in designing compact high pressure engines and boilers for industrial purposes, several of which were used in the various ironworks of South Wales. The application of such an engine to agricultural purposes and, thus, the first placing of a steam engine in the very hub of village life – namely the farmyard – had to wait another eight years, however. In

1812 he built, to the order of Sir Christopher Hawkins of Trewithen, a steam engine expressly designed to power a fixed threshing machine which had, until then, been driven by a team of oxen yoked to roundabout tackle. This engine was no gasping pioneer for it continued in use until 1879 when, fortunately, being recognised for the important relic that it was, it was removed to the Science Museum, South Kensington, where it is still preserved along with the boiler of the second engine of the same kind, made for Lord Dedunstanville of Tehidy Park.

Trevithick proposed, if he did not actually build, a self propelling version of this engine for in a letter he wrote from Camborne (10 March 1812) he remarked to Sir Christopher Hawkins:

'I am now building a portable steam whim on the same plan to go itself from shaft to shaft . . .'

and again, on 26 January 1813 he wrote to Rastrick who built a number of his engines at Stourbridge:

'I wish you to finish that engine with boiler, wheels and everything complete for ploughing and threshing, as shewn in the drawing, unless you can improve on it.'

Such engines as that supplied to Sir Christopher Hawkins were small, weighing about 15 cwt and costing £63, because the threshing machines they were intended to drive were small. Machines for threshing had been the subject of experiment for many years and a workable example had been patented by Andrew Meikle (1719–1811), a Scottish mill-wright, in 1788. Other inventors, including John Balls, a Devon man settled at Hethersett near Norwich, contributed to the reduction of threshers to practical forms but even Balls' machine, patented in 1805, was small and capable of being worked, if need be, by a hand turned handle. Slight though it was of itself, it became important because its inventor's daughter Sarah married the second Richard Garrett of Leiston and became the mother, grandmother, and great grandmother of successive heads of a village factory making threshing machines which, in the succeeding century and a quarter, became celebrated over large areas of the globe.

The spread of the use of machines for threshing, however, was linked more to the vexed question of agricultural wages and employment than to the technical improvement of the machines themselves. Threshing by flail, drudgery though it was, being done in barns, provided employment in adverse weather for the agricultural labourers paid by the day – as opposed to the skilled men, such as horsemen, cowmen and shepherds, commonly paid by the week – who would otherwise have gone home without wages. The introduction of a machine to do this work which represented, in many cases, the defence of a family against destitution, was resented bitterly by the men themselves and was embarked upon only cautiously by farmers and landowners, partly no doubt from fear of the real threat of Luddite reprisals, and partly perhaps, from humane or compassionate motives.

However, the final disposal of Napoleon and the settlement of the state of

Europe by the Congress of Vienna in 1815, again allowed the entry of foreign corn thus bringing down the high prices of the home grown article that had encouraged the ploughing of marginal land which now became progressively less profitable to cultivate. The introduction of the Corn Laws, protecting home production by a sliding scale tariff, secured the position of English grain growers to some extent but arable farming became less prosperous and there was a hardening of attitudes between employers and employed and an increased interest by farmers in the use of machines and steam engines.

The relationships between farmers and the men were not helped by the fact that whereas for some twenty years, since 1795, it had become increasingly the practice to operate the 'Speenhamland' system of augmenting inadequate agricultural wages out of the Poor Rates, the reduced yield of the Poor Rates, consequent upon the reduced annual values of farms, brought about a progressive reduction in such help after about 1815, culminating in the Poor Law Amendment Act of 1834 which abolished outdoor relief of the poor and required those needing help to enter the workhouse. The rumbling discontent amongst agricultural labourers broke into open rural revolt in Kent, Sussex, Hampshire and Wiltshire in the late summer and autumn of 1830 in an outburst of rick burning, machine smashing

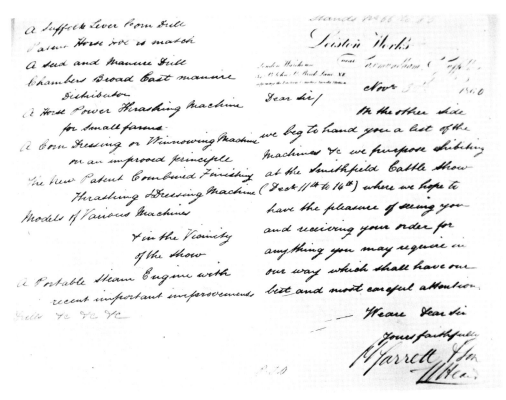

A letter sent out by Richard Garrett & Sons in November 1860 advising clients of their proposed exhibits at the Smithfield Cattle Show that year

and cattle maiming, put down by the authorities at the end of the year with, as the late Tom Rolt described it in *Waterloo Ironworks* 'the legal ferocity which the violence provoked', the leaders being hanged or sentenced to transportation.

This suppression extinguished rural hopes and set off the process of emigration, which became a flood in the second half of the century, to the towns, to the colonies and to the United States. It did, however, give farmers a feeling of greater security against intimidation and gave impetus to experiments in the use of machines, either horse-worked or steam powered.

Though Trevithick, as we have seen, had had some ideas of making his agricultural steam engines portable and possibly self-propelling, and may have reached the point of beginning a prototype, he seems never to have progressed beyond this point. It was the spread of the steam railway, triggered off by the successful opening of the Liverpool & Manchester Railway in 1830, that brought to the countryside the spectacle of the steam locomotive in motion with its train, demonstrating beyond doubt the practicability of steam as a tractive force. The railways, in turn, helped to absorb the village unemployed, to a limited extent in the actual building of railways but much more in the manning of them by plate-layers, crossing keepers, signalmen, constables, porters and carters. Train staff – drivers, firemen and guards – on the whole tended to be townsmen. The 1850s saw the main lines largely complete – in twenty years more the majority of the infilling with branches and secondary lines had been finished, many of them promoted, through mistaken optimism, local pride or the dishonesty of promoters, with little hope of economic return and a future only as picturesque by-ways. Even in the 1860s, so rapid had the evolution of locomotives and carriages been, there was no shortage of obsolete examples which gravitated to a placid survival in the undemanding services on some village branch, a gentle existence amidst the quiet fields and untrafficked skies of Victorian England. How many cottage mantelpieces bore a velvet framed portrait of a young man, awkward in the stiffness of an unaccustomed velveteen uniform and the unnatural rigidity demanded by the slowness of the photographic emulsions of 1865, posed at his first entering the service of the railway company in which he was probably to remain for the next fifty or sixty years?

The men and firms who were making the railway locomotive a practical tool for constant daily use stayed aloof from the needs of the farmer. Just as seed drills, hoes and ploughs remained mostly the wares of the wheel-wright, carpenter and blacksmith, so the main stream of engine builders were content to leave the building of farm engines to small workshops and agricultural implement makers. This trait, in established engineers, of standing aloof from road steamers was noted as early as 1860 by Charles Young in writing his *Economy of Steam Power on Common Roads* when he commented 'engineers, as a body, seem to have been wrapped up in the belief that it was impossible; and they have not only believed it to be so, but have spread and propagated this opinion with great zeal and perseverance'.

The scientific savants of the first half of the nineteenth century had a penchant

The little Brown & May portable used by Roberts, Glyn Bach now restored by Mr Roger Wyeld. (*H. R. Wyeld*)

for sweeping assertions about innovations. Probably the most widely read of these popular scientists was Dr Dionysius Lardner – once described as 'more popular than scientific' – who, pronouncing upon the suggestion of a direct steamship route from Liverpool to New York, said without hesitation 'it was perfectly chimerical! and they might as well talk of making a voyage from New York or Liverpool to the moon'. Two years later the 'Great Western' gave him the lie about the Atlantic crossing but it took another century and a half to go to the moon.

In the face of apathy from the major firms and ridicule from the learned it thus fell to very humble makers to carry on experiments in the use of steam on farms and on the roads.

Cambridge of Market Lavington, Wilts, now remembered, if at all, only as the inventor of the Cambridge, or ring, roller was an early experimenter with portable engines. Another, possibly the first after Trevithick, was Nathan Gough of Salford who essayed a portable engine in 1830. Another early maker, of some success, was Howden of Boston, Lincs who, after building twelve portables, the first in 1839, desisted as he believed the country had become overstocked. The improvement of implements, including the threshing machine and portable engine, was encouraged by the holding of the great annual agricultural shows organised by the Royal Agricultural Society of England, beginning with a show at Oxford in 1839. Their competitive atmosphere and the prominence given to machinery gradually led to improved portable engines but it was not until the sixties that portables and threshers became reliable instruments in wide use, by which time the traction engine and ploughing engine had already appeared tentatively on the scene.

Traction engines, after a hesitant start in Ransome's combined self-propelling engine and thresher on the same chassis (1842) and Robert Willis' 'Farmer's Engine' designed (in 1840) as a road engine per se with the cylinders under the boiler as in a railway locomotive followed, in the 1850s and early 1860s, a deviant line of development, by making common portable engines self-propelling by the addition of a pitch chain and sprocket drive, before settling finally into the mould which is still familiar, having the cylinder behind the chimney and the road wheels driven by gearing.

The 'Farmer's Engine' was a visually neat but, unfortunately, fragile attempt to design an engine specifically for use on farms. It was constructed, for J. R. & A. Ransome of Ipswich, by the firm of E. B. Wilson & Co of Leeds, already celebrated for their railway engines. The designer, Robert Willis, had failed, however, to put enough meat in the parts to stand the shocks to which they were subjected. Though the actual workmanship was good, the high initial cost, coupled with unreliability, destroyed its commercial chances, a combination of factors which may be suspected of having brought to nought many subsequent attempts by other manufacturers. The high initial cost of a traction engine compared with the cost of a comparable sized portable probably directed attention to the cruder but cheaper self-propelling portable engines. A traction engine might cost a 100 per cent more than the corresponding size of portable engine, but making the latter self-propelling added only some 20 per cent to its cost.

The village engine of about 1860 was likely, therefore, to have been either a common portable, moved, when necessary, by horses, or else a self-propelled portable, probably still steered by a horse in shafts but propelled by its own machinery and usually capable of hauling the threshing machine as well. On the other hand very large or well-equipped farms or establishments where expense was not a prime concern of the owner might have a fixed engine as was often the case on the farms of the new class of 'hobby' farmers who, having assembled a large fortune in some other pursuit – perhaps cotton spinning, steel making, brewing or, as in the case of John Joseph Mechi of Tiptree, Essex, from making a patent razor strop – were prepared to dissipate some of it in model farming. Such men were often derided but they played a valuable part in the development of agriculture by bearing, in the course of their hobby, development and experimental costs which could not have been borne by farmers dependent upon their farming alone for a livelihood. Poor Mechi, for example, who began life in poverty as a Italian barber in London before inventing the now forgotten strop which elevated him to the ranks of the wealthy, spent immense sums in fostering agricultural experiments and subsidising inventors until he had lost his entire fortune.

So, apart from such large establishments, where the fixed engine and boiler might be set in a brick-built engine house surrounded by other buildings containing

An early front-steered chain traction engine by Charles Burrell of Thetford, Norfolk. Dating from the 1860s it was still working in its native Norfolk when this photograph was taken early in this century. (*J. L. Middlemiss collection*)

the machines – threshers, root pulpers, provender mills, cake crushers, chaff cutters, pumps or saw-benches – for which, through a system of shafting, pulleys and belts, it had to provide the power, the greater demand was for an engine on wheels. It was a simple and logical progression from this principle of the mobile engine to the idea of having it owned not by the farmer but by an outside contractor who brought it to the farm only as and when needed and by special arrangement. Thus the threshing contractor was added to the village scene which he was to grace or, in a few instances, disgrace, for the next ninety years, some sticking to the one trade but others adding to it that of steam ploughing or, later, steam rolling, with, perhaps, some steam haulage thrown in.

Steam ploughing and steam cultivation, which took place mainly between June and October fitted in nicely with threshing which carried on from October through to the following spring. Attempts to produce a steam propelled plough had been going on since the 1840s. Early examples, such as that patented in 1849, by James Usher, the Edinburgh brewer, relied upon direct traction. That is to say the whole machine propelled itself, or attempted to propel itself, across the field, ploughing or cultivating as it went. Apart from any question of the mechanical soundness of the early designs – and many had weaknesses of layout or construction – they failed as a class because of the relative rarity of days when the soil was dry and firm enough to support their weight. In a few words they dug themselves in. James Boydell attempted to overcome this problem by means of his 'Endless Railway' first patented in principle in 1846 and, in a more practicable form, in 1854. Under his system, an early application of the track-laying principle, large wooden shoes, bearing an iron track, were hung on the periphery of the wheel which thus rode continuously upon the iron track as successive shoes came into contact with the ground. With modern high duty steels the system might have been made a commercial success. As it was, however, many well-qualified engine makers – Bach (of Birmingham), Garrett, Burrell and Tuxford – retired defeated by the metallurgical problems of keeping the shoes economically in repair.

Efforts became centred, therefore, on systems in which the steam engine, or engines, remained on the headlands of the fields and the implement was hauled across by cable. Systems of haulage were invented using, variously, moveable engines at one or both ends of the field or, stationary engines (usually portables) in conjunction with a windlass and a system of rope guides and anchors. The double engine system emerged as the most successful of these and of the double engine systems that of John Fowler was, by the late sixties, the leading make. Nevertheless double engine outfits were expensive and to get the best utilisation from each set it was usual for it to be owned by a contractor, an aspect that slotted in well with threshing by contract.

Hardly had threshing and ploughing contractors become established than they and their unfortunate customers were overtaken by the agricultural depression which clouded the concluding twenty years of the last century. Contrary to what had been predicted, the repeal of the Corn Laws with their protective tariff in the

A 10 NHP double cylinder traction engine of 1869 built by Clayton Shuttleworth & Co of Lincoln (works No 9338) and owned by Henry Smith of Cropwell Drove. (*F. H. Gillford*)

forties had not seen a ruinous decline in the price of home grown corn, because of the rapid expansion of the population of Great Britain and consequent increased demand. It was not, in fact, until the seventies when railways began to open up the true potential of the vast wheatlands of North America and Australia that the rate of increase in imports began to overtake the growth of demand and to depress the prices realised for home grown wheat. Worse was to come, for in 1879 the country had the worst summer in living memory – dull, cloudy and wet throughout the critical months of ripening and harvesting of the wheat crop – so bad, in fact, that many crops rotted as they stood. The Royal Show, held in July at Kilburn, North London was an ocean of mud in which judges, exhibitors and spectators crept about from duck-board to duck-board, machines were sunk in ooze and livestock stood miserably in wretched conditions. The correspondent of the *Engineer* said of the ground:

'. . . it is impossible to move about except on planks, which go squash squash in soft slimy mud at every step. Rheumatism stares you in the face, catarrh peeps round the corner.'

Worse than catarrh threatened farmers. Many could not meet their rent and were evicted, others where reduced to penury by the loss of entire crops and there were many suicides. This disastrous summer of 1879, ruinous in itself to so many farmers, was the precursor of a series of dull, wet summers, none so bad as 1879, but none good for corn-growing. In consequence many areas of ploughed land were turned, or fell, back into pasture and the threshing and ploughing contractors soldiered on, in the reduced demand for their services, using the engines and machines they had had when the depression began.

However, industry prospered and the populations of the industrial towns benefited, by way of cheap food, from the low prices of the lavish imports of foreign wheat. The middle and latter part of the nineteenth century saw the construction or re-construction of innumerable country houses for those made rich by this period of industrial prosperity. In the village where I was born, Leigh, near Tonbridge, Kent, the Hall Place Estate was bought in 1870 by Samuel Morley, the Nottingham hosiery manufacturer, subsequently the first Lord Hollanden. The existing house was demolished, to be superseded by an impressive neo-Tudor mansion in brick, the estate was augmented by the purchase of adjacent lands, the village was rebuilt in stages, a model home farm was established, sewers were installed, an estate waterworks was constructed with its own steam pumping station, a sawmill set up and a gas works created, though it supplied only the house and its appurtenant buildings and not the village. Later a fire brigade was formed for the village. The first fire engine was a Shand Mason manual but the second was a Merryweather steam pumper. With these two appliances the volunteer brigade served the village and its less fortunate neighbouring villages faithfully for many years though as the crew had to be summoned from their daily work and the horses fetched from the home farm, turnouts took some while. It was a village joke that when the brigade was summoned to Larkins Farm, Chiddingstone, about four miles away, sufficient time had elapsed before their arrival for Mrs Day's cook to have made pies for the firemen to eat with their beer.

Like many similar estates, the Hall Place estate underwent a severe contraction of income after the 1914–18 war and successive economies whittled away its self-contained services. The first casualty, in the twenties, was the gas works. In 1931 the Merryweather fire engine was replaced by a trailer pump drawn by a motor fire tender, built by Ray Faircloth, the village wheelwright, upon the chassis of a large Standard motor car, given by Joseph Randerson, the surveyor to Sevenoaks Rural District Council, who lived in the village. The last melancholy duty of the steamer was to pump out the water seal pit of the dismantled gas holder prior to demolition of the under water work. After this, in full working order and having done possibly no more than a couple of weeks steaming, in all, in its whole life it was consigned to Butler, the Tonbridge scrap merchant, for the few pounds that its metal fetched. Soon after that mains water reached the village, the steam pumps were abolished and the whole neat complex – gas works, waterworks, workshops, stores and messroom – lost its purpose, though the shells of the buildings lasted some years more as stores until war damage hastened their end.

Such an estate installation was by no means uncommon and in some places, particularly the North East, where some local nobility were coal-owners, even more elaborate workshop complexes were found. It was the coal on Lord London-derry's estate in Durham which prompted the building of Seaham Harbour as a point of shipment. The need to keep its plant and engines in repair led him to build Seaham Harbour Engine Works and the existence of the well-equipped works led to the actual building of machines and finally, about 1903–12, into the building of steam lorries, a considerable progression from the original estate works.

Not only on the estates of the rich, but also in less exalted ownerships village steam engines might be found. Millers, for instance, who had relied upon water or wind-power alone, in less competitive times, often found it convenient to install an engine to drive a roller mill and widen their scope as did Reuben Rackham when he built the steam powered Deben Roller Mills at Wickham Market, Suffolk, in 1893, the year of one of the best corn harvests on record. The horizontal engine in this mill was locally made by the firm of Whitmore & Binyon at Wickham Market. There had been an earlier steam mill, erected in 1868, using the bricks from the demolition of a four sailed windmill, and there was also, and continues to be, the original Deben Mill, a watermill of great antiquity. An old working mill whether wind, water or steam, is a wonderful place to be in and a great moulder of character and self-discipline, producing men of sensitivity and instinctive culture. Such a one was the late Tom Edward Harris of Denver Mill in Norfolk. Brought up amidst the working of this great tower windmill and its daughter steam mill he developed a feeling for all kinds of machinery and a talent for engineering which led him to add a good engineer's workshop to the facilities of the mills. He was also a gifted model engineer, who made many fine scale models of notable locomotives, a chorister at Ely Cathedral, an accomplished organist and a composer. As a lad, in the first decade of this century, he drove the Mann steam cart owned by his father. When I visited him in 1950 he described how he used to groom this steed:

After I had had my tea in the evening I used often to slip out with a lantern into the engine shed – it was kept in a proper brick engine house with doors – and give the boiler and paintwork a good rub down and wipe over the motion work. The engine was warm, that was easy then you see. Sometimes when I had done I would just sit on the seat – it was warm and comfortable – and take in the sounds and smells, the rumbles from the boiler, the smell of the hot oil and the vibrations of the mill running alongside. I am an old man, a contented man. I have had a happy life. I shall die satisfied because I have fulfilled all my ambitions.

As Tom was almost writing his own epitaph in those reflective words so, as he spoke, he summed up the spirit, even then nearly vanished, of steam in the village.

2. Beating the Corn from the Ear

Threshing near Bildeston, Suffolk about 1920. The tackle was owned by Taylor Bros of Bildeston and the engine is a Garrett 4 NHP compound tractor fitted with a superheater in the chimney base

Two farmers at Chiddingstone, Kent, George Hale and John Abram Day, owned between them a set of steam threshing tackle – a Fowler traction engine and a Marshall 54in threshing machine – with which, apart from threshing their own crops, they undertook similar work, by contract, for other farmers. As both of the owners were friends of our father my brother and I felt a personal interest in this set and it was a matter of excitement whenever it passed through the village.

In those days it was driven by an elderly bearded reprobate known as 'Uncle' Leigh (not to be confused with 'Father' Leigh who was a roads foreman for Sevenoaks Rural District Council) whose son Lew, an ex-sailor, was mate. Uncle, like many threshing drivers, was of chronically short temper and perhaps over partial to his beer. He was, however, good at keeping the engine and machine in repair with minimal facilities. If he had a fault it was perhaps that of hammering the engine rather fast – for its owner's peace of mind – along the hard road, often it must be confessed, to make up time lost by lingering too long at a public house.

During my first day's threshing with this set in the early spring of 1932 at Lower Street Farm, Leigh, a nest of young rats was uncovered in the stack. The ratlings looked so small and innocent that I was misguided enough to reach down to pick one up and was rewarded by having the end of my finger bitten through. Even then farmers were beginning to use motor tractors to drive threshers but the Day and Hale partnership believed in steam and so, because the engine used that day was wearing out, in 1934 they bought a brand new Fowler single cylinder agricultural traction engine, the last one to leave the works. Four years later John Day died and then the war came, hastening in the change-over to tractors, and in 1945, when only eleven years old, this magnificent engine was sold for scrap for only fifteen pounds.

Because we had learned something about threshing from being with that set it was easy to imagine, with the arrogance of youth, that the little knowledge we had accumulated was applicable throughout the country or perhaps more widely but, as I was to find, nothing of the sort was the case even in England whilst in Europe even greater possibilities of diversity existed. George Hambling, the foreman of the boiler shop at Leiston Works, Suffolk, took a holiday in Spain in 1960, when the combine harvester had taken over almost completely in England. He related to me afterwards:

We went through one village and they were threshing with a tractor. I said to the wife 'That's a bit behind the times'. A little later we came across some threshing being done using a steam portable and I thought they were pretty old fashioned. Then we came to a village on a hilltop and they were using a flail . . . well . . . !

There has been no serious use of the flail in Britain during this century though now and again a flail might have been found hanging in a barn. If such a flail was used at all in latter years it would have been only for knocking out perhaps a few beans kept for seed. Before clover hullers came into use for beating out clover seed it was sometimes the practice first to pass the harvested clover plants through an ordinary threshing machine to remove the seed heads from the stalks and afterwards to knock out the seeds from the separated heads by flail on a specially close-boarded floor but I have never seen this done. Others attempted to reset the drum very fine, passing the heads through again, but this wasted the seed and was no use.

Though threshing by flail required little capital equipment it was an expensive method of working. A contributor to *The Times* of 3 January 1851 calculated that, in 1794, when agricultural wages were very low indeed, threshing by the flail cost between two shillings and sixpence and three shillings and fourpence ($12\frac{1}{2}$p and 17p respectively) per quarter of wheat threshed. In 1811 the limits were five and sixpence ($27\frac{1}{2}$p) to seven shillings (35p) and in 1850 were down to an average of about three and sixpence ($17\frac{1}{2}$p), but in that latter year mechanical threshing, by a horseworked machine, cost only one shilling and sevenpence half-penny ($8\frac{1}{8}$p) or, by steam, only sevenpence half-penny ($3\frac{1}{8}$p). By that time there was, of course, little threshing done by flail, though that little persisted throughout the last quarter of the century. My maternal grandmother (born Thirza Jane Hutchins, at Dummer, Hants in 1873) remembered, as a child, seeing men threshing by flail in a barn, though the steam machine was the general rule. What she witnessed was probably the threshing of some choice sample of seed barley or wheat which the grower did not wish to expose to the risk, real or imaginary, of bruising in a machine.

The risk of damage to the grain – very real with early machines – implanted in conservative-minded farmers a distrust of mechanical threshing, not helped by the fact that early threshers, taking the full straw end-on, delivered it in the same battered condition as a modern combine, with the important difference that, whereas combined straw, if not burned on the field, is baled up so that the state of the stalks is, consequently, of no importance, the straw of a century and a quarter ago was sold in bundles, which could be done only with whole straw. Broken straw might be tolerated for home use as bedding or fodder, or for chopping into chaff, but it was of little use for sale or for thatching. To ask whether the machines themselves improved only slowly because demand for them was poor or whether the poor demand was the result not only of the innate resistance – for different reasons – of masters and men to innovation but also of the characteristics of the machines, is to pose a chicken and egg question to which no answer is readily available.

Two factors combined, in the end, to make mechanical threshing more attractive to farmers. One was the designing of threshing machines on wheels, capable of being moved readily from place to place, and the evolution of the portable steam engine as a practical tool. The other was the emergence of contractors willing to undertake threshing by the day or as piece work. As *The Times* remarked (23 July 1857), 'Great value will be found in this arrangement, by which the farmer's

In the generous stackyards of East Anglia and the south Midlands there was plenty of room and big engines were in order. In this picture an 8 NHP single cylinder Garrett owned by G. F. Townsend of Exning, Suffolk, not far from Newmarket, is seen threshing. Note behind the engine chimney the corn sacks piled on a traction wagon

engine can travel with its threshing machine from one homestead, or estate, to another without the assistance of horses'. Farmers then, as now did not care overmuch for the maintenance of machines. Oiling and greasing, if not too frequent or complicated, was just tolerable but the work of running a steam engine – sweeping the flue tubes, washing out the boiler every ten days, taking up big-end and other bearings and seeing to the steam tightness of glands and packings – as well as keeping the threshing drum running sweetly and in balance – were matters they were glad not to have to perform. Besides all this there was the sound economic reason that an engine big enough to run a thresher properly – say an engine of eight nominal horse-power – was too big for most other tasks on the farm such as driving a cake-crusher, a chaff-cutter, a root pulper or a saw-bench for which a six or even a four would have been enough. So a great many farmers, unless in a very large way of business, or unless, again, farming as agents using monies earned by their principal in other pursuits, tended to leave threshing to the contractors and to work such other machines as they had by hand or horse-power. The Royal Agricultural Society, in the councils of which noble lords and the machinery makers had perhaps a rather stronger voice than was warranted by their real importance to farming, deplored this strongly as evidence of old fashioned methods and its judges at the Bury St Edmunds 'Royal' in 1867, proposed that no further horse-worked machines should be accorded trials at Royal Shows. The committee of the Smithfield Show was not so prejudiced, however, and continued to admit horse-worked machines. As late as 1874 Garretts of Leiston, Suffolk, sent a horse-worked thresher to the Smithfield Show by which time horse-powered machines had, more or less, ceased to be manufactured. Nevertheless small horse-powered machines were finally displaced only by the arrival of the small single cylinder internal combustion engine.

Fixed threshers, either horse-worked or driven by fixed engines, lasted longest in the north east of England, where farmers, in the harsher climate of that area, had cattle in yards for more of the year than most farmers elsewhere, preferring to thresh at regular intervals throughout the winter, using up all products as they went, rather than to deal with their whole crop at one time with the aid of a contractor. By contrast, in the marches of the Welsh border where farms were not large and the total cereal crop might make no more than a day's threshing for a small outfit, the scale of the threshing engine and the thresher was adapted to the scope of the work to be done. Such a small scale operation was that of Roberts, Glyn Bach in the hills of Denbighshire, using a little engine built round about 1870 by the long defunct firm of Brown & May of Devizes, Wiltshire. With it he used an equally diminutive threshing machine and also possessed a very small saw-bench. Roberts, Glyn Bach, lived an isolated life in a small farm in a remote valley. When he died his house sank into ruins and the little portable and its attendant thresher and saw-bench rotted away in the undergrowth. As far as the engine was concerned there was eventually a happy ending, for it was purchased by Mr H. R. Wyeld who took it home to Norfolk where it has since been restored in a most careful manner. Roberts' little engine could be conjured up the break-neck roads and the precipitous tracks that were at once the beauty and the bane of his native countryside, where the farmer's horse, as his means of transport, remained a commercial necessity until the road improvements of the last twenty-five years.

The living to be earned from such a small isolated farm as Glyn Bach (Little Glen) – about 30 acres of sparse hill grazing – was frugal indeed. Two or three cows and their calves, some chickens, a pig and maybe a dozen or fifteen sheep constituted the livestock and the arable was a small patch for potatoes, cabbage and cereals. The staples of life on such a farm – bacon, potatoes, bread and butter – were all home-produced. Every penny counted and even thirty years ago it was accounted a luxury to have bacon for breakfast – bread and butter and tea was the norm.

It is said of old Roberts that, having walked to Bettws Yn Rhos (a round trip of about six miles) to do his shopping, he decided on arriving home, that the two old pence he had paid for an ounce of tobacco represented more than he could afford, whereupon he walked there and back again to return the tobacco and have his money back.

Threshing in these hills was a communal affair. As the thresher came round to each of the little farms in turn the neighbours would walk over, after they had attended to their stock, and turn to at pitching, stacking or sacking, usually on a reciprocal basis without payment in cash. The visit of the thresher provided one of the rare opportunities for gregarious work, by contrast with the solitary working lives of most hill farmers, and if the rate of working was limited by the smallness of the engine and the machine no one minded very much.

No such limitations, however, inhibited the contractor working in the South Midlands, the land of large farms, wide firm roads and sound stony stack-yards where big traction engines of seven or eight horse-power, often, in latter years, in retirement from heavy haulage or the fairground, were quite in order and none of the backing, scrubbing and turning, or the tricky siting of the machine with the push-pole was needed that was necessary further north in the tight hilly farms of Cumbria or in the far west in the steep and narrow lanes of Devon and Cornwall. One traction engine manufacturer (Charles Burrell & Sons Ltd, of Thetford, Norfolk) went so far as to design an engine specifically for work in the West Country, only 6ft 3in wide overall, which was dubbed the 'Devonshire' traction engine. Some proprietors in these difficult terrains, such as Sutton & Son of Beckermet, Cumberland (Cumbria) used, in this century, the type of light, fast traction engine known, as a class, as steam tractors and which, because of their smaller size, the Motor Car Act of 1903 permitted to be handled by one man.

The same engine as in the last picture – G. F. Townsend's 8 NHP Garrett – hauling away two traction wagons loaded with threshed wheat. The pictures were taken soon after the engine was new and probably date from the autumn of 1906. Note the chain slung on the leading wagon – useful for pulling out the second wagon to a position where it could be coupled up to the first. The motion work of the engine is covered and it has belly tanks under the boiler because of its intended use for road haulage as well as threshing. The oval licence plate of the Suffolk County Council may be seen on the offside motion cover

Drivers of these engines often performed wonders in coaxing their charges into constricted places. This is what Syd Sutton (the 'son' of Sutton & Son) had to say:

> . . . threshing up here in the Lake District was no easy job; it was not un-common to have to set up in three stack-yards in one day and occasionally move into the fourth for next morning. Most yards were awkward and narrow, as were the approach roads to the farms and sometimes I've had to take off the wheel caps of the machines to pass between dry stone walls because if a cap touched one cobble most likely a few yards of wall would collapse.
>
> Occasionally I had to turn the engine and push with the rear in some of the very difficult yards. On one or two occasions I had to set the engine back-wards to the machine because the gradient of the yard was so steep.

When belted up to drive a full sized threshing machine, the engines, being smaller, had to work very hard to deliver the power output demanded by the machine and consequently needed very careful handling and close attention whereas the larger engines of the Midlands had ample reserves of power and could be left to jog along alone for half an hour at a time whilst the driver attended to the corn sacks or did some other odd job.

Engines and sets working in the Fens of East Anglia, though not faced with hills, also had the problem of narrow roads – the miry tracks and droves which abounded in the Fenland. At St Ives, in the Huntingdonshire fens, the small firm of Fowell & Sons produced traction engines designed especially to cope with such roads with their short awkward turns into fields and farms, reducing the turning circle of their engines by shortening the wheelbase so that the front axle was placed further back under the boiler instead of at the extreme front. The much larger firm of Robeys, in Lincoln, also designed engines with similar characteristics. Road improvement programmes in the Fens, mostly in the last thirty-five years, have put hard surfaces on to most of the once notorious roads, on which, as Harold Darby of Sutton recalled, it might take a substantial part of a winter's day to move the tackle out of one field four miles along the road and into the next:

> It weren't just that the roads were soft – they were so narrow. Oftentimes you couldn't back up to the drum and just take a straight pull on to the road. You had to scheme the engine out first and then rope the drum out and mess about with sling-off chains, and if you weren't careful and tried to do it too fast you'd have it up against the gate post. That weren't all that easy once you were on the drove, some of them were that bad. You might go a bit and then have to drop the drum and go forward with the engine and then rope the drum up to it. By the time you'd done that once or twice the day was slipping by a bit. We used to like it when it was a right hard frost. You could move on that.

My late friend Bob Cheeseman who worked all his life for Chris Lambert of Horsmonden (and for his father, William Lambert, before him) described how he graduated in his teens, in the early years of this century, from mate to driver.

Me and the young governor (Chris) were taking the tackle into a farm Willesley Pound way. The road in was through a wood and that *was* wet. We'd got to go best part of a mile and we couldn't get on even with the paddles on. So we started in roping ourselves along. We'd put a sling chain round a tree and rope ourselves up to that and sometimes we could take the engine and the machine on and sometimes only the engine and we then had to rope the machine up separate. After a bit a message came that the young governor was wanted back at the yard so off he had to go and he said to me you'd better carry on and I'll send old So and So to help you. I carried on, got it in and levelled the thresher and set the engine and he come back and he says 'You seem to be doing alright, you'd best carry on' and that's how I came to drive.

The threshing season started at harvest and went on, weather permitting, throughout the winter but farmers did not care for its straying into the next spring. Fire risk was at a minimum during these four or five months but in an English season never wholly absent. If an outfit was properly set up, with a seventy foot belt from the engine to the machine, inflammable rubbish removed from around the ash pan of the engine, some water kept in the ash pan, a spark arrester fitted to the chimney and care taken in the disposal of hot ash, risks during working hours, even in a dry spell, were minimised. A driver might also turn over a few sods of earth to make a firebreak under the engine and keep a drop of water handy in a bucket. Nevertheless fires did happen from time to time with greater or lesser regret on the part of the owner of the burned property depending upon how well the insurance company paid up. A farmer once remarked to me that the best crop of barley he ever grew in the field we happened to be looking at was the one destroyed by a fire resulting from a hot cinder being dropped by a passing train.

Fear of fire, in the days when the only means of fighting it was a chain of buckets from a pond or stream, was a very real deterrent to the pioneer use of steam driven threshing tackle and one of the reasons why, once the principle of using a travelling set was adopted, stack-yards were often made well away from buildings. In any case the need to store the sheaves in or near a barn vanished once hand-threshing ceased. During the 1939–45 war farmers, at least in the South East, were required to disperse their corn stacks because of the danger from incendiary bombs. The Day and Hale set was pulling in to such an isolated stack at Leigh Park Farm after 'Uncle' Leigh had retired. Lew was driving and Charlie Baldwin was his mate. The ground was soft and a wheel of the drum sunk in. Lew gave the engine a little extra steam to extricate it, one engine wheel spun on the greasy surface and the sharpness of the exhaust threw a hot cinder from the chimney on to the thatch of

Outside Beckermet Station, Cumberland in 1939 Syd Sutton stepped off his own engine (Garrett No 33953 of 1920) to take this photograph. This is the engine with which he did threshing in the constricted stackyards of the surrounding countryside. When he took this picture he was hauling a timber tug. (*S. Sutton*)

the stack which was, before the fire brigade arrived on the spot, burned out. Lew said he had the spark arrester on; he may have done, but he disliked it as it made the engine steam badly by acting as a damper on the draught to the fire.

Threshing, however, was predominantly a job of the damp, windy or frosty months and the dust it created made it a very dirty job. If the wind blew from the machine towards the engine the latter and the driver would be subjected to a continual bombardment of dust, cavings, thistle down, weed seeds and other rubbish that got into the eyes and made its way inside the clothing. This was bad enough on a cold day but in hot weather it induced a particularly prickly state of discomfort. How much dirt was flying about depended upon the crop going through the machine. Possibly beans were the worst, especially if they had been pulled up rather than cut, because of the earth on the roots. But hulling a stack of musty clover ran a close second. There was an added hazard with beans because one would occasionally get carried right round with the drum and be expelled toward the feeder with all the venom imparted by the beater bars travelling at about five and a half thousand feet per minute. Such a high velocity bean was an uncomfortable projectile and to guard against it many threshing men used to rig up a temporary protective hood made of a sheep hurdle covered by a piece of tarpaulin. The dry fluff from inside the bean pods used to blow about and stick to anything wet or oily. You could start the day with a nicely cleaned and oiled engine and finish it with the engine looking really woolly. But if the engine did not get the rubbish, so long as there was a breeze someone had to have it. If not the engine driver, then the pitchers or the men on the straw stack were the recipients.

The worst job of all was working under the thresher, keeping the bottom free, raking over the cavings sieve and seeing that the straw fed properly into the tier and elevator which passed it up to the men building the straw stack. On the whole, apart from blown rubbish, the latter had the best of it. By the time the straw reached them the dust had been knocked out of it and there were no rats or mice. In the days of steam threshing many farm men wore leggings which helped to stop dust and the occasional mouse from going up their trouser legs but those who wore no leggings would often tie their trouser legs into their calves with a strap or binder twine. This also helped to keep the cold out when the weather was bad, for threshing went on during heavy frost though it stopped for rain.

It was usual for only the driver and mate to be hired out with the machine though, as in Cumberland, sometimes the hire included three, in which case the third man acted as bond cutter whilst the mate did the feeding. Besides these three jobs there were needed two pitchers on the corn stacks (or three, if the stack was large), two men to build the straw stacks, a bottom man to keep the bottom of the machine clear, a sackman to attend to the corn sacks, weigh them and move them into the barn or granary, and a carter to keep the engine supplied with coal and water and remove the bagged chaff to the loft. These latter two were usually the

A load of chaff en route to the Newmarket racing stables from Takeley chaff mill in the mid-twenties. The wagon is Foden No 11260 owned by Frederick Darby & Sons of Sutton (near Ely). The close sheeting with tarpaulins is to protect the load from sparks. The wagon was new in December 1923

first and second horsemen on a large farm. They helped each other out and had some help, as a rule, from the driver.

It was the customer's duty to provide these extra men, though it was not always convenient for him to do so. The custom arose, therefore, of threshing machines having more or less regular 'followers', men who followed it from farm to farm in the hope of being employed as casual labour. Sometimes, like the enginemen, they had their own cycles to ride home on, sometimes they walked, or in some instances, slept rough in a barn or under the machine. On the road they rode or walked behind, or perhaps rode on the thresher. Sometimes a trusted regular would be allowed a spell steering the engine.

If such casual workers sustained an injury there was much claim and counter claim as to who should bear the cost of compensation. The engine owner would claim, rightly, that they did not work for him, but, on the other hand, farmers often used devious devices to make it appear that this was so. A favourite was to hand the engine driver the money to be paid out to them so that they always received their pay from one of the contractor's men and would, with complete honesty, swear to this in court.

My grandmother used to recall one such old casual who worked on the farms around Dummer (near Basingstoke), where her father was an estate blacksmith, in the eighties. During the winter he stayed in the workhouse but came out to work at haymaking and threshing, sleeping wherever he could find shelter. Her mother used to give him meals from time to time and grandmother remembered him eating a herring. Too long-sighted to see the bones, he used to pick the fish up and eat from one end to the other avoiding only the backbone.

The late P. A. Mathieson recalled, in 1961, some of the happy times he had had with these wandering threshing gangs in Lincolnshire, nearly forty years before, and the laughs they had had together. As one of them remarked, they could afford to laugh, because a laugh cost nothing.

There was Fred, who stuttered badly and was courting a widow named Kate. Ted the feeder made a butt of him over this with the popular song 'K-K-Katie', and no sooner had the thatch been removed than Ted would look up at the rick, and his voice raised in song would proclaim 'She's the only g-g-girl that I adore'.

Fred wore a multitude of clothes: cord trousers, waistcoat and two jackets. At five o'clock he would look at his watch, point to the whistle and nod his head; the time was always correct, it was verified by Big Ben on his crystal set, to which Ted would make the reply that it was not the same time as on his set. On one unforgettable day Fred took off both jackets; he left his cord waistcoat on, but at knocking off time he caused much merriment by looking for it. Tom the engine driver pointed out that he had got it on, and so greatly relieved Fred's feelings.

Another tramp thresher was Henry the Drover. He loved traction engines and threshing machines, and the rattle of the tackle going by or the hum of the drum always brought him along. It was Henry's great ambition to own a threshing set. The engine was to be a Clayton, and he carried around a catalogue of this famous firm's engines and a coloured plate of an agricultural engine. These he had obtained by going to the works at Lincoln and asking for them, but what Messrs Clayton thought of their potential customer is best left to conjecture.

Billy the bond cutter was a lovable lad. He disappeared each spring for employment as a showman's labourer, and he travelled with a set of steam gallopers. As a steerer on the big Burrell, or driver of the centre-engine, organ-man, money-taker, nothing came amiss to Billy. He came back to his village each winter but of his travels he said nothing, knowing well he would not be believed.

Ben, who stacked the straw, claimed to be deaf; only to give himself away when the farmer said quietly, 'Come to the house for some beer.' Down the ladder came Ben, and 'Ah,' said the farmer, 'he heard that.' A large stone jar was carried on the straw-elevator for filling when the farmer provided beer or cider.

The water-cart man was usually the farm carter, who with a pair of horses brought the water to the engine. On one occasion the carter was gone a long time, so Tom the engine-driver gave a blast on the whistle. The carter, who was called 'Bawley', a nickname he had earned by his loud voice, came at last with his load of water, and angrily he addressed Tom: 'You tell your boss to buy a new engine; that-un does nowt else but suck up water; next time you come here threshing I will tell our "gaffer" to build the ricks on the bank of the river.' 'No need to do that,' said Tom. 'Your mouth full will be enough.'

Edwin Foden Forth (b. 1904) was the engine-driving son of a driver so dedicated to his craft that he gave his son the name of his favourite make of engine as a second christian name. The Forths worked in the East Yorkshire wolds where the wind could be so cutting that '. . . in a stiff north-easterly freezing wind, such as we get on the Yorkshire wolds, I have had the steam gauge freeze up whilst threshing'. In his part of the country custom required the farmer to provide meals for the driver and mate – a mixed blessing. At the right farms it was good food and plenty of it, but at others conditions were best summed up by another man's comment, 'I'd always prefer to be shot rather than poisoned'.

The driver's day did not end when the last stack was finished for he probably had to move the tackle on to the next farm and set the drum ready for a start the next morning. In times of hard frost when all the ground was frozen hard this might be a cold job but otherwise not too bad but when the ground was soft it was a different story. After a finish about 4.15 or 4.30, just as the light began to fail, the driver had to knuckle to with his mate, pack up and get out on to the road, travel whatever distance had to be covered and set the machine ready for work next day. To quote Edwin Forth again:

He might have to move several miles to the next farm where there was a bad road and stackyard, (or) maybe into a field. This meant putting all the spuds on and probably having to haul the machine with the wire rope. This was bad enough in daylight but imagine having to do it in the dark with the wheels full of mud which kept dropping down one's sleeves when groping about finding the pin holes and, as sometimes happened, with it pouring with rain.

Notwithstanding the snags, the engine driver's pride in, and devotion to, his trade could become obsessive. The story has been related by Iain Inglis of 'Black Tam' who worked with a Burrell engine and a drum (or a 'mill' in Scotland) for Davidson Bros. in the Scottish lowlands not far from Glasgow. Indifferent alike to personal comfort or, it must be admitted, bodily cleanliness, he pandered to the requirements of his charge by cleaning, oiling, adjusting the engine and drum and storing up in an encyclopaedic memory the location of awkward hills, bad bridges and suitable water pick-up points – in the latter case distinguishing those that were bad and, hence, to be avoided – and the other minutae which made for the sound running of the engine. He was, like Michael Reynold's ideal engineman (*Stationary Engine Driving*, 1880) 'full of expedients, full of opinions, full of facts and wants to be nipping the evil in the bud'. The day came when his employers decided to make the change to diesel. He was shown the new tractor that was to replace his engine. After surveying the disgusting device in silence for a second or two, he turned and said 'Gimmee mah cards.' Taking cards and wages he slung his old coat over his shoulder and tramped off back towards the railway station and Glasgow, never to set foot in the yard again.

Engine drivers and their mates were early morning men and always about betimes, by dint of greater or lesser personal effort according to the temperament of the individual or how strong the pull of the tap room fire had been the night before. Those who liked to sleep in their own beds often faced a lengthy ride on a bicycle to get to their work. Some firms, whose sets travelled widely, provided living wagons for the crews to sleep in during the week but spending the chilly autumn nights in these little boxes was an austere existence compared with going home even if, in some cases, home itself was not synonymous with high living. Conversely, however, since it was the practice to arrive at the engine at 6.30 am, a five mile cycle ride beforehand meant early rising for the man who lived at home.

The night before, the engine would have been left with a banked fire, and a full boiler, the ashpan damper would have been shut and a steel lid put on the chimney top. Often it was possible to arrange for one of the farm horse-men, who arrived in the stable at 6 am, to take off the lid and open the ashpan door but if it could not be arranged – because the site was isolated or because the engine crew had got at loggerheads with the waggoners – then the mate had to get up half an hour earlier still.

The first job of the driver – the mate unsheeted the drum – was to clean the fire running the poker the whole length of the space between each bar to make sure the air space was clear, and to remove any clinker found by means of the long handled clinkering shovel. When the weather was dry it was sensible to douse any hot clinkers with a bucket of water – no point in taking needless chances. If the coal had been bad the day before or the work was to be very heavy, as when, for example, a chaff cutter was included in the outfit, it might be necessary to sweep the fire-tubes but often it was enough to do this once at weekends and once midweek.

The engine would have been covered overnight with a canvas sheet of a size to cover the motion works, gearing, boiler front and man-stand. When cleaning the fire this was rolled back only as far as the breast plate, just enough, in fact, to get it out of the way of the firehole door. Leaving it over the engine work kept off any dust coming from the firehole, protected the bright work from the damp dawn air and kept in the heat whilst the engine was warming up. Once the fire was going well the driver would take off the cover and oil up the engine. If they were to move on the road that day he would oil up the road gearing, axles, steering and turn-table but if they were to thresh where they were he would oil the engine work only and then turn-to with the mate in oiling the drum. Most drivers and mates had a set routine of their own as to who oiled what. Oiling the shaker cranks was always the mate's job as it meant crawling awkwardly inside the machine, and so was the oiling of the top of the elevator which involved some climbing, but the Day and Hale thresher, a Marshall, had ball bearings which greatly reduced the amount of oiling needed.

Just before seven, with all this finished, the main band, slipped off overnight, would be put on and there would be enough pressure to tick the engine over to warm it up and brighten the fire. Day and Hale's engine was of six nominal horse-power, in the traction engine builder's curious rating, but it was a Fowler, a first class make, and could run the drum at one hundred pounds' pressure of steam or a little over. The speed was increased as the pressure rose until the drum was revolving at eleven hundred revolutions a minute, at which speed it was held by the governor fitted to the engine. When it was running Uncle would examine the belts. The drive from the engine to the main shaft of the machine drove the drum direct but the subsidiary parts were worked by secondary belts off the main shaft – the shakers, riddle crank, bottom fan and awner – whilst the elevator, top fan and corn screen were driven by tertiary belts. Slipping or failure of a belt meant the stopping of the function it powered and soon led to a jamming up of the machine if not spotted. Even if noticed in time it meant a tiresome stoppage. Uncle was very fussy about the belts, therefore, and, like most drivers, acquired the knack of noting, sub-consciously, the click-clacking pattern of sound made by belt fasteners or buckles passing over the pulleys.

Such an inspection never took him long and when it was complete, about 7 am, work would begin. Lew stood in the feeding box on top of the drum, receiving the sheaves from the band-cutter and feeding them into the drum, barley generally end-on but wheat lengthwise. The empty drum revolving at working speed had a higher note but when adroitly fed it settled down to a deeper, vibratory hum. The more regular the hum and the steadier the engine beat the better the feeder could be said to be, for lumpy feeding meant uneven work for the engine and a consequently irregular exhaust note as the governor had constantly to adjust the supply of steam to keep pace with the fluctuating load. Cantankerous though many drivers were, they would, as a rule, give each man on the thresher a short break in turn – feeder, band-cutter and sackman. The recognised and safe place for a quick 'pull' on a cigarette was on the man-stand of the engine.

A threshing outfit at work in the tentative sunlight of early November was, in many ways, the epitome of steam in the village. The hesitant rays struck through the mist and the branches of trees to rebound off the bright brass of the boiler band or off the glistening cross-head, loping back and forth. The dust motes whirled in the shafts of light, and here and there a fugitive wisp of steam escaped from the engine. Then there was the urgent hum and regular beat, the nattering, each in its own time but none in time with the other, of the belt fasteners passing over the pulleys and of the cranks and shakers, and the sight of the deceptively leisurely swing of the sheaf from the first pitcher to the second, from the second to the band-cutter on the platform of the machine, from the band-cutter to the feeder and then at the other end the steady issue of straw on to the elevator and from the elevator to the straw stack. The straw stack was the old hand's job – none of the pitching upwards, the dragging out of embedded sheaves that went with the corn stack – but, with the skill of experience, the steady teasing-out of the clean straw into a tidy and stable straw rick. A badly built rick, too narrow at the base, or unevenly laid on, was an abomination, leaning awkwardly on its wooden crutches until the reproach was removed by the steady winter appetite of the stockyards, cowsheds and stable for straw.

Lunch, at threshing, was not the genteel title of the midday meal but of the mid-morning break, usually from nine to half-past, which divided the morning. Bread and cheese, bacon sandwiches, a slice of fat salt pork, a raw onion, more rarely a tomato, were the staples washed down with cold tea brought from home in a bottle. Clear glass whisky bottles were popular but Uncle used an embossed bottle that had once contained Rose's lime juice. Rarely, at the onset of the season, there might be a ridge cucumber but bought cucumbers very seldom. As was once commented to me by a driver 'I can get my indigestion without buying it.' Dinner time came from one to two made up of the same viands as had been brought out at lunch. Many of the farm men went home to dinner. During this time the driver and mate would repeat the oiling routine, check round the belts and cut away any straw that had wound itself round the rotating parts of the elevator – such straw could be so tight that it was almost like cutting through wood. Work stopped at five but even without a watch one could tell finishing time was approaching by the slowing down of the engine as pressure was reduced by the driver filling up the boiler in preparation for banking down for the night.

Threshing started about late September, soon after the end of harvest but not usually immediately on it for farmers liked to give the corn a little while in the stack before threshing it to allow the air to circulate through it, dry out any residue of dampness and harden the grain. In the Weald of Kent, where farmers often also had hops or apples which they liked to get well in hand before getting committed to the further task of threshing, it tended to start later by a couple of weeks. Two-thirds would be over by the end of the year and most of the rest, unless halted by bad weather, by the end of February, though sluggards or unfortunates, or the chronically bad payers, might have a stack or two left even as late as May. What corn they got from such a stack they received by courtesy of the rats and mice which would have moved in and multiplied on a considerable scale. A hundred and twenty-five days work in a season was considered a poor showing, a hundred and fifty about satisfactory and more than that great good fortune. As a days output of threshed corn might be of the order of four tons these one hundred and fifty days represented some six hundred tons.

In the latter days of steam threshing it was mostly done by hiring out the engine, machine, elevator, driver and mate by the day. Less than half a day counted as a half day and over half a day as a whole day. This is how my friend Stan Jacques, driving Arnold's Burrell 'The Empress' could manage, when working in the spring or autumn for small farmers, having only one stack, to get in three 'half-days' a day. Sometimes, however, threshing was taken by the hundredweight of grain threshed. In the thirties a set and its two men might be hired out for two to three pounds a working day, the farmer finding the coal. It must be remembered that all bargains were individual and the truth about prices never much talked about though there was a fair traffic in lies – farmers about how little they could get the work done for and contractors (to each other) about the magnitude of the prices they received. What the men got in the thirties varied with their experience and status, the district and the employer – Suffolk was one of the lowest wage areas and Surrey one of the best. The range for drivers was probably from about thirty-eight shillings to fifty shillings a week (£1.90 to £2.50) whilst mates probably ranged from twenty-eight shillings to thirty-eight shillings (£1.40 to £1.90) – it is very difficult to be sure for scientific statistics simply do not exist and the human memory is a jade.

Whatever the rate of wages when at work there was always the problem of the 'off-season' – for the engine owner as well as his men. Some enginemen had the good fortune to work for humane, if thrifty, men and spent the summers on their employer's farm. Others were not so fortunate and were laid off for the summer, taking casual farm work when available – hoeing roots, singling beet, haymaking and harvesting in the due seasons. In the arable areas of eastern England and the east Midlands many threshing men went steam ploughing during the summer, the recognised season for it, and threshed in the autumn and winter. Others took jobs as steam roller drivers or drove for travelling showmen. During the summer, too, any repairs needed to the engine or machine would be done and perhaps the drum repainted. Because this kind of thing made drivers resourceful many of the miscellaneous repair jobs about the farm tended to come their way – the odd bolt required in a plough, the board on a barn or tile on a roof. Thatched roofs though, on the whole, were left to the thatcher, perhaps because techniques were required that linked the work to that of the craftsman rather than of the handyman. Yet this ancient craft, too, had its links with threshing for thatching straw needed to be long, unbroken and neatly tied, to achieve which virtues the co-operation of the threshing men – particularly the feeder – was needed. Wheat straw was that generally used for thatching. Oat straw was softer and, in any case, in demand for feeding whilst barley straw, being fed end-on into the drum to achieve optimum results in the threshing, was usually too bruised.

Whilst only reasonable care was needed to produce a sample of straw for thatching a stack or the occasional cartshed, thatchers and their clients demanded a rather better sample for use on farmhouses and cottages with the bundles selected and knocked up by hand. Because this could be tedious and time consuming, in Devon, where straw for thatching was in considerable demand, one of the Murch family, threshing machine owners at Umberleigh, devised a straw comber for attachment to the back end of the threshing machine designed to arrange the straw into the consistent and orderly bundles beloved of the thatcher.

Fires in thatch which were caused, or alleged to have been caused, by sparks from a traction engine were a bane to owners and men alike but the actual danger, seen in retrospect, can be overstated. The glowing particles above the chimney of an engine in motion might have looked spectacular in the dusk or in darkness but were mostly so small that they cooled within a foot or two of the chimney top. It was when sizeable cinders were ejected that trouble had to be looked for. A spark arrestor in position mostly checked these but even if it was not in place, as, it must be admitted, often it was not, only gross overloading or careless driving would have created a serious fire risk on the level or on slight gradients. Steep hills, however, were another matter and heavy collar work on a real gradient could produce a pyrotechnic display with resultant fire risks in dry weather. Threshing was a task mainly for autumn or winter, seasons when bone dry conditions are, to say the least, not prevalent in an average year. Risk times were, therefore, mainly in the tail end of the season, May or perhaps even the odd stack or two in June, or when threshing began soon after harvest.

The practice of having the threshing set actually in the harvest field, threshing the sheaves as they were gathered, was used in dryer areas abroad, combine harvesting being the logical culmination of this, but the practice never took root in Britain. Nor did the British farmer, unlike his American counterpart, take to the idea of harvesting by steam, despite the efforts of engine manufacturers to foster the idea of hauling a self-binding reaper by a steam tractor. Whether or not this reluctance was the result of innate conservatism, lack of capital, fear of fire, or a distrust of the capacity of an average harvest field to take the weight of a steam tractor is an open question. One of the most disinterested pioneers who experimented in this field was the late John Collings (1882–1950) of Bacton Hall, near Norwich. A man of some means, he was also a sound practical engineer who established, on his estate, an engineering workshop of a size and level of equipment sufficient to enable him to build there a traction engine and two steam tractors of his own design, intended to test the practicability of steam for general farm tasks. He used one or other of these on the farm land of his own estate from the time they were built (the third was finished in 1915), until the decline of his health and capabilities in the mid nineteen forties but never convinced others by his example. His efforts to foster the use of steam in the fields led him to be looked upon as something of a crank and, indeed, there was a strong element of the eccentric in his make-up. A handsome man, full bearded, he preferred to busy himself with engines and machines and the improvement of agriculture when his private means were sufficient to have enabled him to live a life of scholarly ease. His end was sad. He never married and after the death of his parents he lived alone at Bacton Hall becoming more and more of a recluse, neglecting the once handsome gardens and failing to keep even the roofs in repair. One by one the rooms became uninhabitable until he was reduced to living in a single room in which one morning he was found dead mainly as a result of his self-neglect.

No greater success attended the direct traction experiment of John Goddard (1854–1952) of Tunstall, Suffolk, who bought, in 1919, a 'Suffolk Punch' steam-driven agricultural tractor, built by the nearby firm of Richard Garrett & Sons Ltd of Leiston. Practical experience over a couple of seasons convinced him that useful though the engine was at threshing, its operating cost and size made it out of the question for ploughing or harvesting. John, moreover, was no diehard. He lived and farmed until he was over ninety and readily adopted the internal combustion tractor late in life. He did not give up farming until he was ninety-eight and his interest in experiment and progressive practice which had led him to buy the 'Suffolk Punch' never dimmed. John Goddard was, unlike John Collings, a robust, practical farmer and far from a visionary, but neither in his hands nor those of John Collings did the steam tractor achieve any commercial foothold in either ploughing or in the harvest field.

3. The Steam Plough

Between 1830 and 1840 the rapid propagation of railways, depending for power upon the locomotive, demonstrated, beyond any reasonable doubt, that not only was steam traction capable of handling the loads and speeds required of it but that it was cheaper and immeasurably more reliable than haulage by fixed engines and ropes, except upon the most extreme gradients. In addition to this, after the success of Timothy Hackworth in setting steam haulage of the Stockton & Darlington coal trains on a sound footing and the handling of passenger traffic of the Liverpool

The patent steam self-propelling cultivator designed and made by Thomas Rickett of the Castle Foundry, Buckingham in 1858

& Manchester Railway by steam locomotive even the most rabid opponents of steam hardly bothered to canvass the claims of animal traction.

It is not to be wondered at, therefore, that the inevitable deduction came to be made that steam might provide a cheaper alternative to the horse in that most basic of human activities, the ploughing of the soil to receive seed, nor that, after the dismal performances of fixed engines and rope haulage on railways, the hope of inventors should have been centred on direct traction, after the example of the railway locomotive, with a traction engine drawing its plough across the field or, as an alternative, having a plough or cultivator mounted directly upon it, a system which, in this country, has been employed with great success upon motor tractors in modern times.

Though the early direct traction experiments experienced grievous inadequacies in the action, design and construction of their machinery, there can be little doubt that, had the system itself had in it the essentials of success, the purely technical snags would have been overcome, as they were with railway locomotives. The fundamental problems, however, were size and weight, in relation to British field conditions. We will return to this point in a moment but before looking at this negative aspect it may be worth considering the development of direct traction ploughing by steam in North America where it was done very successfully, particularly in the great central wheatlands. In these areas the landholdings had none of the contorted interlocked nature so often exhibited by the plan of an English farm. Instead the land was allocated in large consolidated blocks, frequently plain rectangles or squares given over in whole or greater part to arable and extending to many hundreds, where not thousands, of acres. When ploughing such a block an engine might be able to go a mile – and sometimes much more – before it had to turn about and return. Thus, although the headland was large it was a small percentage of the total of the block and was further reduced by the passage of the engine and plough along it, at completion, at right angles to the original direction of ploughing. Moreover the land itself, because of the predominantly dry autumn climate, was very firm underfoot.

English field conditions were an almost total contrast. Sometimes, it is true, the land in autumn is dry and very firm so that a heavy engine may travel up and down it without fear of damage to the soil or of sinking in. Often, however, it is not. Few, indeed, would be rash enough to describe English weather as predictable. This problem of ground-bearing weight, however, might possibly have been solved. James Boydell (who died in 1862) came near to solving it with his track-laying wheel only to be defeated because contemporary metallurgy could not offer him an iron simultaneously hard enough and sufficiently ductile to stand up to the wear and tear. Field size in relation to engine dimensions was not solved. Too much time was spent and too much land consumed in attempting to plough by direct steam traction in the English fields because of the short length of pull between turning the engine at each end of the field. It was bad luck that in the Fens, where water was plentiful, fields large and rectangular, and the direct ploughing engine and cultivator most likely to succeed on that score, the load bearing capacity of the soil should have been one of the lowest in the country.

There was no shortage, however, of early attempts to achieve a satisfactory direct ploughing or cultivating machine. The majority did not progress beyond a patent or a model. However, the machine designed by James Usher, the Edinburgh brewer, in 1849, was actually constructed and tried in South Scotland and at least one example of that by Thomas Ricketts (of Castle Foundry, Buckingham) was completed. The most sustained effort was probably that of the Canadian, Robert Romaine, to whose designs at least three diggers were made. The first, made under the sponsorship of Alderman J. J. Mechi, of Tiptree Hall, Essex, was built in 1853. The second was made in Canada and sent to the Paris Exhibition of 1855 and the third and, probably, the last was made by William Crosskill of Beverley, Yorks in 1857. Only the latter was self-propelling, the two earlier examples being hauled by horses though having steam machinery to do the cultivating. Mostly these machines were condemned by their own mechanical inadequacies but if these alone had not been enough the practical problems of operation would still have been severe enough to have inhibited their use.

Later three men shared the honour of reducing the steam digging machine to a workable form: Thomas Darby of Pleshey, Essex, Thomas Cooper of Great Ryburgh, Norfolk, and Frank Proctor who worked in conjunction with Burrells at Thetford. Earlier Darby diggers were elaborate and heavy machines with double

How 'roundabout' cable ploughing worked – a wheel mounted double winding drum in the gateway belted up to the portable engine and the moving rope carried to the distant plough by a series of rope porters and moveable anchors

boilers, similar to the Fairlie locomotives still extant on the Festiniog railway in Wales, each with its own smoke-box and chimney. For travelling on the road the axles swivelled round to be at right angles to the longitudinal centre line of the boiler but in the field they were parallel with it. Later examples had the digging attachment arranged so that it could be fitted to the rear of a normal traction engine. Steam diggers were fitted with multi-tined forks and, by an ingenious mechanical action imitated the action of the human arms in digging. When carefully driven a traction mounted digger could do excellent cultivation and, by backing up to hedgerows, dig virtually every part of a field, but real commercial acceptance eluded steam diggers. According to Ronald Clark, Darby sold about thirty of his broadside diggers over a period of some twenty years but then redesigned his machine with rotary tines. A digger was a more complex machine than the robust cable operated ploughing gear, more limited by ground conditions and needing plenty of maintenance, hence not many buyers were prepared to humour its limitations, though good work was done by those who did, and many who saw it displayed intense enthusiasm. One such wrote to Thomas Darby 'When I was at your's, you asked me to let you know what my opinion was of your steam digger. I beg to say I consider it a first rate implement and one that must succeed and I hope realise you a good fortune'. The late Sidney Darby once told Ronald Clark that over £100,000 was sunk into developing his father's diggers without his achieving commercial success. R. C. Stebbing, whose father farmed at Earls

On a fine March morning, in 1907, when already thirty-nine years old, W. G. Fairhead's pair of 14 NHP Fowler ploughers (nos 3051 and 3052) paused for the late Major Ind to photograph them at Ardleigh, Essex

A Burrell 'short chain' ploughing engine (No 801 of 1878), in 1911 outside Manor Farm, Little Thurlow, Suffolk. Its owner was G. Bedford of Little Bradley, Suffolk

Colne, Essex, saw a broadside digger, owned by a Mr Moss of Kelvedon, at work in the first decade of this century but it was about the last in East Anglia and was scrapped soon afterwards.

The lack of success of direct traction gave encouragement to the rope haulage experimenters. Initially, if one ignores the technical and constructional differences of the various items of plant, the rope hauliers were divided between those who stationed a windlass and its power source (which was often a portable steam engine but sometimes a horse-worked capstan) at a static point and used a system of anchors, either permanent or temporary, to guide the power of the moving rope to where it was needed, and those who placed the engine and windlass upon a common chassis which was moved up one headland as the work advanced, the rope passing round a moveable anchor or a series of fixed anchors on the opposite headland.

The most vociferous advocate of the static engine system was William Smith of Little Woolston, Bucks, a farmer of an inventive mind, who devised a system of using what generally became known as 'roundabout tackle' and designed his own cultivator to go with it. Billy Smith believed in the use of the cultivator ie an implement with multiple tines which were drawn through the soil, stirring it up, rather than the plough. James and Frederick Howard, the implement makers, of Bedford, to whom he licenced the making of machinery under his patents, being plough makers, understandably did not share his antipathy toward that implement and advised its use with steam tackle. Since the redoubtable Billy was no man to yield an inch in his views, wordy public squabbles went on between him, Howards, Fowlers and the respective supporters of the three principal protagonists. Contrary to Smith's expectations and, in some ways, seen in retrospect, to justice Fowler was awarded, in preference to him, the coveted prize of £500, at the Royal Show at Chester in 1858, as the first man to make ploughing by steam cheaper than horse ploughing. This incensed Smith who kept up a battle with the RASE of greater or lesser intensity, for a period of some forty years. He accused the RASE of being in league with the plough makers and said they had used 'a mere dodge to withhold the money and favour the old plough makers'. By the 1890s he was claiming not merely the original £500 but compound interest in addition, bringing his claim to over £4,000 which, needless to say, he never received.

Smith, however, had no monopoly of invective. The judges of the Royal Show at Salisbury in 1857 where a public trial was made of various systems of steam ploughing, must have encountered a powerful tirade from one of the competitors, J. A. Williams, to have prompted them to write in their report:

Mr J. A. Williams' system was anything but satisfactory in results. The judges regret to be compelled to add that the extreme discourtesy of his language and conduct towards themselves rendered their duties in the inspection of his work painful and unpleasant in a manner they never before had occasion to experience. . . .

The Victorians never shirked controversy in print and the spectacle of eminent men slogging it out in the columns of *The Engineer* or *Engineering* probably caused them less surprise than it would have done today. Ploughing controversy came to a head after the Newcastle Ploughing Trials, held in connection with the Royal Show of 1864. By this time roundabout tackle was becoming eclipsed by double engine tackle in which two self-moving engines, each equipped with winding gear pulled the plough back and forth across the field. John Fowler (1826–1864) had, by sheer merit, attained great prominence in the design both of the implements and of the engine systems, but there were runners up, notably the small firm of W. & P. A. Savory of High Orchard Ironworks, Gloucester, whose patents were bought by Garretts of Leiston, Suffolk, in 1864. As a Garrett-built set was not ready in time for the Newcastle Trial one was sent that had actually been made by Savorys. This performed well but was outshone, in the estimation of the judges, by a Fowler set using his clip drum system, which was actually invented by C. Algernon Clarke. Whereas with most double engine systems one engine pulled in whilst the other rested, the clip drum system allowed both engines to pull by having a continuous rope which passed round and off each engine drum each of which was fitted with a series of patent clips round its perimeter to grip the rope and transmit power to it as the drum revolved. It was an ingenious system but it was an abberation on the part of Fowler who normally designed intensely practical tackle, for its successful use needed engine crews trained to the precision of a Royal Tournament team. The prize-winning Fowler engines had subsequently a very short life of only two years. The judges might not have been expected to know that, though, as they had the benefit of the advice of that eminent engineer David Kinnear Clark, as one of their number, they might have been expected to have had an inkling but they could have avoided the infantile assumptions as to the cost of annual maintenance which they actually adopted, namely merely to take $17\frac{1}{2}$ per cent per annum of the selling price. To assume, thus, that a cheap machine would cost less to keep in repair than a dearer one seems, to say the least, to be going against probability.

So incensed were the Garretts that they withdrew from any further participation in RASE trials as explained in an immensely long letter of controlled but withering anger, written by the third Richard Garrett and published in *The Engineer* on 14 October 1864, part of which is given below.

We protested against the awards of the judges, at Newcastle, as soon as they were published, because we considered that in making those awards, they 'took no notice of the main points in which our engines and tackle are manifestly superior'; a careful consideration of their report has confirmed us in this opinion. We were well aware that competing as we did with engines manufactured in the ordinary course of trade, and which had been through some six months severe work . . . we should not stand in a good position with reference to the consumption of fuel, when compared with the performance of 'racing engines' manufactured expressly for competition.

Our experience in steam cultivation has, however, shown us that 'consumption of fuel' is by no means the most important point to be considered by employers of steam cultivating machinery, and we were rash enough to anticipate that some other elements would be taken into consideration by the judges in arriving at their final decision. We believe the question of 'wear and tear' with reference to the means employed for hauling the implement, stands uppermost in the minds of those men who have had any lengthened practical experience with steam cultivating machinery, and we are convinced that the capability of performing a large amount of work in a given time will be considered a very important point before steam will be generally adopted in preference to horse labour in the cultivation of the soil. A careful perusal of the judges' report will show that, in making their awards at Newcastle they were mainly guided by the consumption of fuel; thus reducing the whole trial to a simple test of the engines and boilers; no attempt was made to arrive at the comparative merits of the various systems brought under their notice in other more important points.

A Darby broadside digger

With regard to the 'wear and tear' a paragraph attached to the tabular statement in page 397 of the Society's journal speaks for itself:

'The same figures were adopted for "wear and tear", and interest as in the Worcester report, viz, $12\frac{1}{2}$ per cent for "wear and tear", and 5 per cent for interest, divided over 200 days.'

With the following competitors before them, viz: 1st, Fowler's well-known system, with 14-horse power engine, and self-moving anchor; 2nd, Fowler's double engine system, 'the chief novelty of the show'; 3rd, Savory's engine, with two winding drums and self-moving anchor, the first engine made on this principle. And, 4th, our double engines on Savory's principle, introduced at the Worcester show; the judges surely cannot wish it to be understood that no one had the advantage in this most important point.

Did the simple rule of three, adopted at Worcester, apply to all equitably and justly? If so, the matter might have been settled by simply taking the selling price at which each apparatus was entered in the Society's catalogue without going through the farce of a trial.

Do the consulting engineers of the Society endorse this? We are under the impression that the judges did not feel competent, with the opportunities afforded them, of forming an opinion on the subject, and, consequently, they get out of the difficulty by applying to 'novelties' they had never before seen 'the same figures as in the Worcester report'. Can anything be imagined more unjust to the competitors, or more likely to mislead the public?

With reference to the capability of getting over a large amount of work, we are aware that to make good-looking work with the plough, it must not travel beyond a certain speed. With the cultivator the case is different, and we see no reason why twenty to thirty acres of land may not be cultivated in a day with Savory's engines.

On reference to page 401 of the Society's journal it will be seen that we were working at the rate of 17.77 acres per ten hours with two twelve horse-power engines, the price of which was £1,028 10s. Fowler's two nominal seven horse-power engines costing £1,034, worked at the rate of 13.58 acres in the same time: while Fowler's ordinary fourteen horse-power engines, with travelling anchor worked at the rate of 8.37 acres per day. Should this count for nothing? The judges think it ought, and, instead of giving us any credit for this performance, they say, in a paragraph on page 402 of their Journal, 'Notwithstanding the excessive pace, the consumption of fuel was enormous' (not so much, however, as with Fowler's single engine system), from which we gather that, with the excessive pace, they expected a reduced consumption! This is scarcely to be credited in these days of blockade runners and limited mail trains.

We still adhere to our protest, and maintain that the judges at the Newcastle trials did not ascertain the relative merits of the competing systems of steam cultivation, as regards wear and tear; that they did not give due consideration to the capability of performing a large amount of work in a given time; nor to the facility for moving the tackle from place to place, and setting down to work; on which points we also contend that Savory's patent engines, as manufactured by us, are manifestly superior to any others.

Fowler's clip drum engines did not deserve to win at Newcastle but, in the wider view, his basic double engine system and his implements, notably the balance plough and the improvement, made to it after his death by his associates, the anti-balance plough, formed the bedrock of steam ploughing practice as exemplified by the tackles made by his own firm, by McLarens, by Burrells and by Aveling & Porter. Fowler himself lost his life in the hunting field in the autumn of 1864 but the firm he had founded in Leeds was carried on ably by David Grieg and Robert Eddison who had been his associates.

Fowler owed his pre-eminence not only to the excellence, the clip drum apart, of the plant he made but also to the fact that he was the first man to demonstrate, in a trial before impartial judges, at Chester Royal in 1858, that mechanical ploughing used in suitable situations cost less than horse ploughing. The saving, however, was based upon not less than 200 working days in a year, a target quite beyond the annual requirements of most British landowners or farmers considered

Manufacturers, such as Garretts, with no stake in making cable ploughing engines, made valiant efforts to sell steam tractors for direct traction ploughing. This is Garrett 3 NHP tractor No 25399 (1906) giving a ploughing demonstration near Leiston. The wide rear wheels are to lighten the weight per square inch on the soil and the angle rims on the front wheels are to improve the steering by preventing slipping sideways

singly. In practice few contractors achieved it either but that is another matter. Apart from the question of intensity of use there was also the high initial cost of a steam ploughing set (£1,000 to £1,100) to be considered. The combination of the two factors made ownership of steam ploughing equipment an ideal field of enterprise for contractors who bought and operated the machinery and provided the crews together with coal and consumable stores but looked to the farmer to cart water, a system which continued as long as steam ploughing by contract.

In the early days of steam ploughing – the latter half of the eighteen sixties and most of the seventies – much of the contracting was done by steam ploughing companies, the capital of which was mostly provided partly by farmers and landowners or partly, it seems, by the steam plough makers taking equity instead of cash for the equipment they supplied, or granting extended credit on mortgage of the undertaking. Such a method of ownership necessitated control of the actual operations by managers who doubtless often had, as managers in such situations are prone to do, nine fingers for the firm and one for themselves. This probably answered well enough while a modest degree of prosperity reigned. It came under pressure, however, as the prosperity of arable farming declined with the seventies and fell into disarray with the onset of the agricultural depression at the end of the decade. Many farmers were ruined, as has been noted, by the disastrous summer of 1879 and their default pulled the ploughing companies down with them. Of course many individuals who were contracting also went to the wall, but most weathered out the depression, whereas larger companies virtually disappeared.

For the next twenty years steam ploughing remained a depressed trade, soldiering on, year after year, like threshing, with the same engines and much of the same equipment, though there was a certain amount of chopping and changing as work fluctuated between different parts of the country or individuals died, retired or failed. Orders for new engines for the home market all but disappeared.

Hard times for the owners were mirrored in hard lives for the men. The work was arduous and the daily hours long even when there was a good season. A bad season meant fewer working days or fewer men employed, perhaps to the extent that one set in five or so would never leave the yard. A good year for the steam ploughing contractor was a summer when the ground was dry and 'coulter-bending' hard, when not only was ploughing and cultivating very hard on the horses but also the prospects of a good harvest encouraged the farmer to incur the extra expense of having the steam plough in. A wet summer meant easy working for the horses, the prospect of grain losses at harvest and poor conditions underfoot for ploughing engines. In such a year many a farmer was inclined to turn his sovereigns over and put them back in his pocket to the detriment of the steam ploughmen.

In the early days, before the invention of the anti-balance plough, its predecessor, the balance plough, had a tendency to 'run out of the work' when driven fast, unless set deep. As both owner and men were paid by the acre the plough was invariably driven as fast as the engines could move it and consequently had to be set deep. In a shallow soil this could be too deep and result in sub-soil being brought to the surface, damaging fertility, as a consequence of which the steam plough acquired a bad name so that farmers often preferred the tined cultivator which could be driven as fast as possible without detriment to the work. The rule for cultivating was twice over, the second run at right angles to the first.

Early in the year there would be cultivation of fallows, followed, as soon as the hay crop was off them, by the breaking up, in mid to late June and through July, of such old hay bottoms as were marked down for cultivation. At such times the ploughmen would work from dawn till sunset, eating food brought to them in the field by the cook-boy. One driver remarked that they would 'get up at four in the morning, work till ten at night and then fall asleep on the grass'. The late Charles Stewart, chief engineer of the Eddison Steam Rolling Co, which began as a steam ploughing concern in 1868 and kept its steam ploughing gear until after the 1914–18 war summed up the life of the men he had known when, in his eighties, he wrote:

My happiest memories are of steam ploughmen – what men! Bank down at night, usually after dark, when one driver, unable to see his mate at the other end of the field signalled 'Stop pulling in', by whistle. Up before dawn, the foreman on the plough, a toot on the whistle and the slack of the rope taking up the five furrow plough and slowly moving away from the engine. With a single-cylinder one could hear the bark of the exhaust a mile away as the plough passed over the field. Then, with a good gang, as soon as the rope ceased leaving the drum, the driver at our end would give the foreman time to turn the plough and then very gently let in his clutch and watch the tension on the wire. Immediately he could see and feel the plough moving, open the throttle and see the drum take the strain. The only types I can think of as resembling these ploughmen were the iron men in our wooden ships.

A steam ploughing crew consisted, as a rule, of five – a foreman, the second man, who was a driver, a third man (the spare driver), a ploughman and a cook. Unless at work in their village of origin the crew would live, during the season – March to November – in a five berth living wagon, equipped with bunks, lockers, a cooking stove and a table. These were supplied by Fowlers and the other ploughing engine makers – who were never important numerically – and were designed for the purpose with high wheels and storage boxes beneath. The one at the rear was usually called the 'back box' and that entered between the front and rear wheels the 'belly box'. These housed tools and stores and tins of oil. Older wagons had the door in the centre of the front like a gipsy wagon and often had a clerestory roof (or 'mollycroft') but later ones generally had the door in the near side and a plain elliptical roof covered in curved corrugated iron which kept out the rain efficiently but made them hot in summer.

The arrival of the ploughing engines in a village was undoubtedly an event. By comparison with the threshing engine, which was so familiar a sight, the ploughers were vast. On the road the loads they hauled were so puny for the power of the engines that they were never put to spectacular performances and were fairly quiet when travelling. One engine, as a rule, took along the tackle and the other the living wagon and water cart. The word had usually passed round the village as to which farmer was having them in and, provided school did not interfere, they were likely to attract a boy following to see how the problems of entry to the field were tackled – the awkward gate, the narrow culvert or the overhanging branches. Steam ploughmen had a short way with awkward trees, by using two hooks, a long chain and a sharp pull with the engine. Especially in the great arable and potato areas of East Anglia, Lincolnshire and the East Midlands, where villages were very closely linked to farming and alternative employments were few, working on the railway or with ploughing or threshing tackle represented the most promising alternatives to working on a farm, and doubtless a number of the boys who watched the ploughmen so avidly aspired to join them in due time.

Unlike the people of the fairs who carried with them the aloofness and faint air of mystery of the true nomad the steam plough people were known to be basically their own folk even if their base was twenty miles away. On the other hand the

Harold Darby (right) standing in front of his father's 5 NHP Burrell tractor whilst hauling sugar beet in the twenties.

ploughmen were far enough from home and well enough paid to be men off the domestic leash, particularly the younger ones. Some found their freedom in the beer they could afford. Others liked to cultivate a Don Juan reputation. Doubtless actual achievements fell short of the boasting but equally it is certain that the arrival of three or four lusty young men into the shut-in atmosphere of a village gave the local girls some relief from the tedium of always having to flirt with the same lads.

At one time steam plough drivers, like railway engine drivers, affected moleskin trousers, slop jackets and flat hats but the engineman's customary blue jacket and trousers took over quite soon. My grandmother remembered seeing moleskin trousers when she was a child in the eighties but my late friend Charles Hooker, some ten years younger, assured me that they had gone by his time ie the nineties. The steam ploughing crew were undoubtedly better off than the run of farm men; at about the turn of the century Eddison's ploughing engine drivers received fifteen shillings (75p) a week plus an acreage payment of about four old pence an acre of work done, paid at the end of the season to the gang as a whole. Daily output would vary, of course, but three thousand acres might be done in a season producing fifty pounds in bonus money to be shared among the crew, of which the leading driver might get ten, the foreman rather more and the boy-cook a good deal less. At this they were very substantially better off than the farm labourers who were earning about twelve shillings (60p) a week.

In this and in their usurping of the position of horsemen the steam ploughmen represented a challenge to the social order of the village. The steam plough was the first farm machine to displace the horse. Earlier machines, such as threshers, had begun actually by increasing the employment of horses through horse powers and the subsequent displacement of horses from this work by the steam engine had represented merely a reversion and not an encroachment. To see, however, a steam machine at plough, that time honoured task of the horse and horseman, around which such lore was centred, was a blow. Attending on the early steam ploughing sets was a duty looked upon by the horsemen with more antipathy than when they had to serve the steam thresher and the dislike was scarcely diminished by the fact that those who manned this interloper equalled or excelled them in pay.

For a bachelor with no home ties life with a ploughing set had much to commend it. Accommodation was free, the pay good, food cheap and his personal outgoings limited to whatever he chose to spend on clothes, beer and tobacco. For a married man things were a little different, as most of his summer was spent away from home, so that unless the set happened to be working virtually on his own doorstep he could spend only Saturday and Sunday nights in his own bed and that only if the set was within walking or, later, cycling distance of home. If he used the train it had to be at his own expense, which most chose to avoid and it usually meant returning on Sunday as there was not often a train early enough on a Monday morning to get him to work by starting time. So, for much of the summer, his wife would find herself a grass-widow, coping by herself with cottage, family and

The prototype Garrett 'Suffolk Punch' (No 32974), similar to that owned by John Goddard, ploughing under test in July 1917

garden. Home life in many nineteenth century cottage homes could be hard but the companionship of the conjugal couch and the benefits of home cooking were alleviations which the steam ploughman was denied. His diet when at work was monotonous – a good deal of cheese, bacon, which did not 'go off' as readily as meat, some eggs and potatoes and large quantities of bread, with some butter and perhaps jam if he had a liking for it. The staple beverage was tea, hot or cold, with or without milk, supplemented with beer or cider. Water was not popular as it was often suspect unless boiled. Eggs, milk and sometimes beer or cider, might be given by a generous farmer, and eggs were often scrounged by one device or another from mean farmers. Even if paid for, eggs and milk were cheap at the farm.

The cook-boy cleaned the wagon, cooked breakfast, and took meals to the men in the field during the day. He also did any shopping required, which could mean a long walk, fetched drinking water, and if he was intelligent and keen to get on, endeavoured to get himself initiated into the work of the set, standing on an engine and watching the driver or riding on the implement. As he learned he might be allowed to drive an engine for a while under the eye of the foreman or the second man or even steer on the road, but the initiative rested with the lad. If he did not bother to learn when he had the opportunity then he made no progress in the craft.

Ploughing was something which completely took over certain men, the lore woven into the fabric of their lives. Such a one had probably begun as a cook-boy at the age of thirteen or fourteen, absorbing like a sponge all the knowledge that had come his way – how to splice a rope or to set out a field and assess its area, how many tines to put in the cultivator, how – and this was very important – to avoid getting at loggerheads with a difficult farmer, how, again, to humour the prejudices of the customer who, seeing the steam plough once a year, reckoned that he knew more about how the job should be done than the man who had spent fifty years thinking of little else. The old men who were foremen of sets in the declining years of steam ploughing in the mid-thirties had, quite probably, been boy-cooks in the early eighteen seventies and carried, in their heads, the history of steam ploughing in their area over the preceding sixty years.

Each set required only one foreman, however, and the others did not need to have the same knowledge of the trade, though some, obviously, were foremen in the making. The ploughman needed an eye for how to plough and some aptitude for working with machinery whilst the two drivers, provided they had the basic knowledge of how to manage a steam engine, soon acquired the dexterity which made for smooth working in the ploughing team. Such men often doubled up steam ploughing in the summer with driving a threshing set or being second man on one in the winter or, with firms such as Eddison, took to roller driving in the days when water-bound road surfaces required the stone to be laid in the wet winter season.

The threshing and ploughing seasons interlaced very well, one following the other in a most convenient fashion, and in consequence some plough owners were also threshing people but it was not invariably so and there were other ploughing

A typical steam ploughman and one of the last ploughing engines supplied for use in Great Britain – Mr W. Jackson's 18 NHP Class AA7 Fowler compound No 14726, at Toppesfield, Essex, in the same hands continuously since it was new. (*B. J. Finch*)

firms that did not touch threshing or, if they touched it, merely dabbled. There were other tasks, however, besides threshing, which were undertaken by a ploughing contractor. Dredging beds of lakes, ponds and watercourses was one such task. For this a heavy steel dredging scoop, with a front cutting edge, was drawn across the pond bed by one engine, the other merely drawing back the empty scoop. Another type of work undertaken was mole-draining. John Fowler's first interest, in fact, was in mole-draining as a means of reclaiming water-logged land in Ireland and his other inventions followed on from it. The mole plough was a wheeled implement having a single narrow vertical blade, with the plane of the blade in the line of travel, carrying at its foot a torpedo shaped mole. When the blade was drawn through the soil the mole pressed back the sub-soil in its passage so as to form a small waterway, the depth of which was determined by the setting of the blade. Mole ploughs are still in use and machines based on a modification of the principle are used to lay water mains, cables and land drains. Provided there were water courses into which the mole drains could discharge their water, mole drainage was an effective way of reclaiming land rendered derelict through lack of drainage.

Cultivation by steam could also play its part in bringing back into cultivation land which had become derelict through simple neglect. During the agricultural depression of the last century much arable land was allowed to fall back into rough grazing, ringed with overgrown hedges, beset with thickets of blackberry, gorse or hawthorn and infested with rabbits. Much the same thing happened again, a couple of generations later, between the wars in this century. During the 1914–18 war much such overgrown land was cleaned and returned to cultivation by the use of steam tackle and especially by the use of the steam drawn cultivator. Bigger trees had to be pulled out by the roots by use of the wire rope and chains before cultivation, but the cultivator or 'scuffler' as steam ploughmen often called it, was a big enough and heavy enough implement to tackle gorse, brambles or small saplings. Riding the implement through such terrain was a hazardous undertaking made more so if a strand of barbed wire happened to be draped undetected in the undergrowth. Passing over the cultivator this could lacerate the steerer or pull him off the implement or both. Long trailing brambles were a menace too and to guard against long brambles or wire a vertical cutter bar could be mounted on the cultivator rather as was done on military motor vehicles to protect the driver from trap wires.

The cultivator was always a rough ride even on open ground and clearing undergrowth made it even more hazardous. There was the possibility, furthermore, of grubbing up a wasp nest or a nest of wild bees. When that happened it really was a case of 'look out'. Worse still was a hornet's nest but, thankfully, they were very rare. During the 1914–18 war, the last boom time in steam cultivation, the large demand for it, coupled with the loss of men to the armed forces, meant that some engines were in the care of men who would not, in other times, have been given the job. The absolute solecism for a driver and the one most calculated to hurt the ploughman was for one engine to start pulling back, because of mistake or impatience, before the other had stopped pulling in. Quite apart from the risk of damage to the plant there was a strong chance the man on the implement might be flung into the air. If his luck was in he might land on the ground beside it, which was bad enough, but if it was out he would fall back on the implement or in its path, with the probability of dire consequences.

Steam ploughing contractors founded the Steam Cultivation Development Association in 1915, with John Allen of Oxford, a noted owner, in the chair. Perhaps because of this but also because of his wide experience in steam cultivation he was appointed an adviser to the Food Production Department. As the Germans' submarine campaign went on and the need to produce more food at home became more pressing it was Allen who pointed out the important part steam ploughing sets were playing, not only in doing their normal peacetime work but also in taking on a considerable further acreage formerly done by the horses which had since been taken into military use and in the reclamation of derelict land. Because of the importance of this work and the great age of much of the equipment with which it was being undertaken he was able to persuade the government that the

Ploughing on a dull day with plenty of smoke. Taylors BB 1 No 15226. (*B. J. Finch*)

Ministry of Munitions should put in hand with Fowlers, in 1917, the construction of sixty-five pairs of modern compound ploughing engines for use in home agriculture, most of which were delivered, unfortunately, only as the war ended. The end of the boom in steam cultivation did not coincide exactly with the end of the war but by 1920 falling prices and rising costs had priced out much of the marginal land pressed into cultivation during the war and thereafter there was a steady contraction of arable acreage so that after 1920 steam cultivation was hard pressed on this score. This in itself would have been setback enough but it coincided with the resurgence of direct traction ploughing in which the ubiquitous Fordson tractor played a prominent part making the plight of steam ploughing firms very hard.

Interest in direct ploughing had, in fact, been undergoing resuscitation attempts ever since the beginning of the new century both by those steam engine builders who had no stake in the cable cultivation market and hoped to gain one by selling steam tractors for direct ploughing and also by some more disinterested non-commercial experimenters including the late John Maris Collings, of Bacton Hall, Norfolk (whom we have met in Chapter 2) who built his own steam tractors in the estate works and used them for ploughing, reaping and other tasks on the estate.

Probably the most determined attempt by a commercial builder was that made by Richard Garrett & Son Ltd, of Leiston, Suffolk when they designed their 'Suffolk Punch' steam tractor equipped with a driving position at the front and Ackermann type steering as in a motor car. This did remarkably well at direct ploughing and had the Fordson tractor never been invented might possibly have ushered in a new phase of steam cultivation. As it was the Fordson tractor at about half its weight and needing no water to be carted to it in the field killed it off almost as it was born. The use of steam cable tackle, curiously enough, though severely contracted has never quite died out and there is little doubt that as these words are written, in the autumn of 1976 here and there in the arable areas of East Anglia steam ploughing engines are at work.

No steam ploughing was done in my home village in my time nor for ten or twelve years before. The local owners of ploughing engines were Brotherwoods of Tonbridge and their firm had gone before 1914. Thomas Wood & Son, on the chalk fifteen miles north of us, kept their ploughing tackle, including a modern compound set bought in the war, into the 1940s whilst Chris Lambert at Hors-monden kept his engines till he died in 1954, though they did little work, if any, after the war. East Kent, however, with a far higher proportion of arable land kept steam going much longer. Clark Maylam & Co of Lenham, Pouts of Whitstable, the Wingham Engineering Co near Canterbury, Links and Blacklocks on Romney Marsh kept going through the twenties and thirties and Blacklocks and Links, at least, until the fifties. The Blacklock engines were used solely on their owner's land and were beautifully kept by a father and son team. When old Mr Blacklock died the spirit went out of the use of the engines and after a certain amount of tentative use his son had them summarily cut up on the very threshold of the preservation

A set of tackle owned by the late John Patten of Little Hadham, Herts preparing to move from one job to the next in October 1959 when their owner had only a few months to live. The nearer engine is Fowler No 15364 and the other is No 15365, named *Windsor* and *Sandringham* respectively, a pair of Ministry of Munitions engines delivered in 1919. (*B. J. Finch*)

era. The Link Bros were less precipitate and their last pair of engines, after lying disused for a while, were rescued and restored.

The fascination of the steam plough is elusive of definition. For me it has been largely a spectator sport. I was never lucky enough to encounter single cylinder engines at work whose exhaust note, when pulling hard, could be heard two or three miles away. I have heard only modern (ie twentieth century) compounds whose exhaust was quieter and economy greater. But it was not the size or the sound of the engines, the chutter of the exhaust or the plume of steam from the safety valve as they ended a pull which solely cast the spell. The hiss of the bright steel rope in the furrow, the sibilant progress of the plough, turning six or eight furrows in its passing, left fragrant with new turned earth, the flock of gulls or rooks scavenging the new furrows were each a part of a spectacular scene. Jack Wharton, who worked with steam ploughs in his youth, recalled what it was like 'to stand in front of the wagon in the dew of a sunlit summer dawn, and take in the smell of the turned earth, fresh trampled grass, a drift of coal smoke from the near engine and a whiff of frying bacon from the door of the wagon.' Ploughing was a hard craft but it had its rewards.

4. Good Fortune and Bad

The fortunes of the threshing and ploughing contractors, of course, rose or fell with those of the farming community. During the great depression of the 1880s and 1890s they soldiered on as well as they were able, seldom buying new engines and machines and making do with what they had, plagued by bad debts and slow payers. When times improved, in the first twenty years of this century, there was a period of renewal, followed, with the inevitability of night following day, by another period of retrenchment as far as engines were concerned (for a fair number of modern threshers were put to work) between the wars. When times were bad they had to cut costs wherever they could, not only in renewals, but also in wages and other expenditure. Most regarded boiler insurance as a luxury they could not afford and, since the compulsory inspections required, in the case of industrial boilers, by the Factory Acts, did not apply to agricultural engines, inspection as a rule meant a look-over by the owner or his fitter or a village repairer or, perhaps, none at all. Undoubtedly some of these people were experienced and sagacious men able to notice and prevent incipient trouble. In the case of others, lack of knowledge, carelessness, avarice or fear of giving offence sometimes led to highly defective engines being put to work. Because of the greater strains imposed upon the boiler by ploughing, engines engaged in this work were more prone to violent damage than threshing engines. During the 1939–45 war John

Mole draining at Wimbish, Essex with Fowler Class BB 1 ploughing engine (No 15226) owned by Taylor Bros of Wimbish. (*B. J. Finch*)

Downs, whom we shall meet again when talking about village fairs, drove an engine for the Essex War Agricultural Executive Committee. One of the men who worked with him was Wally French whose skin John described as 'blotched and marked all over like a Dalmatian.' The source of Wally's curious complexion was the scalding he had received when he was involved, at Cressing near Braintree, in the explosion of the boiler of a ploughing engine owned by Charles Brown and his mother Mrs S. A. Brown, of Coggeshall, who carried on a business as plough- ing contractors. The accident happened after the end of the 1918 ploughing season on 7 November, when the engine, a Fowler, was engaged in mole draining. Built in 1877 it had had a new firebox in 1904 and had been patched and repaired in its other parts but the boiler was not insured and was not under inspection either by an insurance company or by any other competent engineer. The morning of 7 November passed uneventfully. Wally French and a second man, Ernest Norfolk, were managing the mole plough, Charles Brown was driving the engine in question and Mr South, the farmer, was carting water with a water cart drawn by two of his farm horses.

About noon Charles Brown had just pulled the plough up close to his engine and was waiting for the second engine, at the opposite end of the field, to begin the pull back. Mr South had backed his water cart up to the tender of the engine and was filling its tank through a hose. Charles Brown, who had just topped up the boiler with water, was on the footplate of the engine. A second later he was on the ground ten yards behind it. The front end of the engine had been shattered by the explosion of the boiler. The rear wheels and axle, tender and the new firebox remained where they had stood before the explosion, the actual plate of the boiler barrel was flattened and flung with other debris fifteen feet to the left of the engine whilst thirty yards in front were the smoke-box, cylinder and perch bracket. Ernest Norfolk was still standing, but in a state of shock, supporting himself on his right leg by holding on to the plough with one sound arm. His left leg and right arm were both broken. Wally French was badly scalded. South was unhurt but his horses had bolted and he had stopped them only with the greatest difficulty.

At the subsequent Board of Trade enquiry it was revealed that not only was the boiler barrel badly weakened by corrosion and local stressing but it was being worked at 135lb per square inch pressure, although when new, forty-one years before, it had been intended only for 100 psi. A crack had appeared in the boiler a few days before the explosion but instead of effecting a proper repair Charles Brown had merely stopped the leak by caulking it up with a chisel. The inspector commented 'Great ignorance and recklessness seem to have been displayed in the management of the engine and boiler. . . . Many owners of agricultural engines and boilers often fail in this respect and incur unknown and unnecessary risks themselves and expose others to the same risks. . . .'

Even when an engine was under inspection it was no infallible protection and for an account of a potential disaster as a result of ignorant driving Edwin Forth may be quoted once more:

Cultivating with Taylor Bros Fowler engines, No 15227 (nearest camera) and No 15226 (in the distance). The driver is the late Olly Taylor (second from left). (*B. J. Finch*)

Father and I were once called to a farm where they had a Mann's agricultural tractor. 'Something was wrong with the engine.' When we arrived on the farm where they were threshing . . . father took one look at the steam gauge and shouted to the driver to get the pump and injector hard on if he didn't want a quick trip to heaven. When eventually things got cooled down we made a few enquiries and it appeared that the boiler inspector had been a few days previously and given it a hydraulic test. He had left the removal of the plugs in the safety valve to the driver who, being a novice, hadn't done so. The needle on the steam gauge was up at the stop and not a whimper at the safety valves.

More mishaps happened to threshing sets, however, by running off the road than by boiler accidents. Sometimes nothing more calamitous than a heavy and awkward job of recovery from a hole or ditch was the result but, as happened at Cringleford near Norwich in 1901, sometimes real disaster resulted.

A threshing set consisting of an eight horse-power Burrell traction engine, thresher and straw pitcher was crossing the narrow bridge over the River Yare

Mr Hegbin's Burrell traction and threshing machine after having fallen through the parapet of Cringleford Bridge (Norwich) in September 1901. (*R. H. Clark collection*)

between the villages of Easton and Cringleford, on opposite banks. In drawing to his nearside to avoid an oncoming horse and trap the steersman caused a front wheel of the engine to collide with one of the massive spur stones set in the roadway to protect the parapets from damage by traffic. The shock snapped a link in the offside steering chain, the forecarriage was driven back to full left hand lock so that the engine collided with the parapet, part of which it demolished, and fell upside-down into the river killing both the men trapped on the footplate. A baker, Herbert Flatman, who had followed the Burrell and its loads on to the bridge, had the harrowing experience of witnessing the accident from a distance of a few feet and of seeing the two men, with whom, about a minute before, he had been talking, carried to their deaths. He called to the driver of the trap, a Mr Wade, the unwitting cause of the accident, that he was afraid, as he put it, that 'they were all in', in reply to which Wade said 'Dear me', raised his hands in token horror and drove on, probably the ultimate in callousness.

Aside from all these mishaps there was the menace of the law itself and of the police who endeavoured – over zealously in the opinion of most threshing men – to enforce it. The common causes of offence were the emission of dark smoke, the

The stout man in the trilby hat is Fred Hann, driver of the unidentified Eddison-owned roller in the background. Fred, known to his mates as 'Cadger' for fairly obvious reasons, was noted for his voracious appetite and original culinary methods. A piece of fat bacon, potatoes and a cow cabbage boiled up together in a bucket are said to have been stock ingredients of Fred's diet

blowing off of steam on the highway, failure to give precedence of passage to horses, or failing to leave a spark arrestor in position. In the case of the first two of these it was virtually impossible not to offend involuntarily at some time or the other and if one was unfortunate enough to be within sight of a constable at the time a charge was the likely result, more particularly if on strange territory. Village policemen, living in a small community, knew each of their flock by name and were aware of, or liked to think they knew, the shortcomings of each. Sometimes they were, perhaps, more in the dark than they imagined themselves to be. Be that as it may, an occasional minor offence committed with a threshing engine in its home village might expect to be met, unless the constable had other scores to settle, with nothing more dire than a warning. Once further afield, however, the case was different. Men working with a thresher and living in a caravan were, to most village constables, travelling men, having no local roots, and, therefore, liable to be lumped into the common category of suspicious characters along with gypsies, tinkers, organ grinders, travelling showmen, buskers and hawkers. To a policeman in this frame of mind it was not so much a question of whether or not they were offenders as of 'catching them at it'. The dice were loaded further against enginemen by the fact that many magistrates were drawn from the ranks of the retired or well-to-do middle class – users of carriage horses or of horses for riding – with antipathy towards traction engines. Typically, at Hythe, Kent in 1907, Captain Mansell commented, apropos of nothing in particular, in a traction engine case; 'Traction engines are a great nuisance at the best of times . . .' and his fellow magistrate, Captain Baldwin added 'Traction engines are horrible things'. Such comments cannot have gone far to convince the defendent that the hearing was impartial.

It was my great good fortune to have known, in the latter years of her life, Mabel White, the widow of Doctor James White, a petroleum technologist much older than her, who had entered his profession as assistant to 'Paraffin' Young, the man who in the 1860s pioneered the extraction of paraffin from the shales of Derbyshire and south west Scotland. Her father was Jesse Ellis, of Maidstone, who carried on a business in his home town from the 1870s until 1907, as the owner of traction engines, rollers and ploughing engines. A stern, unbending and probably, by current standards, a ruthless man he encountered many troubles in the course of his business life and was involved in a number of adventures many of which Mabel was able to recall with verve and precision.

One of his engines, as I have recounted in *The Age of the Traction Engine*, blew up one night in 1880 in the centre of Maidstone but there were many other incidents less dramatic. On one occasion the firm became embroiled with the Chief Constable of Kent. Manktelow and Boarer, the two drivers involved were old retainers of Jesse Ellis and well-known to Mabel White. Tom Boarer, in particular, was a well-known character in Maidstone. When young he had lost a hand in an accident but nevertheless managed to drive a traction engine using one hand and a stump. Cross-grained and monosyllabic though Tom could be he had qualities of integrity and self-reliance which appealed to her father for whom he worked continuously for something like forty years, until the two of them were both old men. The encounter with the Chief Constable happened near 'The Bull' at East Farleigh on a short level stretch of road between two hills. The two drivers stopped their engines in response to a signal to do so from the Chief Constable's coachman. Not unnaturally the two engines, the fires brightened by the sharpened exhaust during the climbing of the hill they had just surmounted, began to blow off steam at the safety valves. This, under the irrational provisions of the Locomotive Act, was an offence and the Chief Constable sent his man forward with an instruction to them to stop it. Manktelow succeeded, probably because his engine had an injector and he was able to put in some boiler feed water without running the engine. Old Tom was not so lucky and could not stop his engine blowing off so a prosecution resulted. It began as the Chief Constable versus Jesse Ellis & Co but on the magistrates indicating that they found the offence proven, the firm indicated that they then wished it to proceed, as the Act allowed, as the case of Jesse Ellis & Co versus the two drivers, both of whom were convicted and fined. Mabel White believed that her father later reimbursed them the fines and had proceeded against them only because the bench tended to be more lenient toward employees than an employer. Not every employer would have done the same and drivers resented the facility afforded by the law to the owner of an offending engine, if the offence was established against him, to continue the case as between him and his driver. A fine of a pound upon an owner with an income of five hundred pounds a year might have been an annoyance but to a driver earning seventy pounds it was a disaster.

Two Fowler road locomotives and their trains pause for water in a scene of quiet rurality during the War Office trials of road engines in 1903–4.

Most threshing drivers were capable, though often difficult, men but, of course, their levels of competence varied, often in direct proportion to the capabilities of their employer. Like attracts like and the kind of tackle owner who was interested only in getting by in any makeshift fashion generally recruited men already of like character or, if not like it when taken on, content to be moulded to his ways. The soundest judges of a man were his peers – the other threshing drivers of the area. They would know, and few better, the shortcomings, if any, and the subterfuges he used to cover them and in any kind of discussion between a gathering of threshing men there would be a nice diversity of professional opinions on the way things ought to be done. To each, naturally, his own methods were the only sound ones. All of this, of course, was very right and proper – the very stuff of which pride in one's craft was made and part of the secret of contentment. Not all drivers were of this calibre, however, and there were others of less admirable character. My friend Esmond Kimbell was a threshing driver for several years and an owner and a contractor for many more. He once wrote:

Of course, there were also some dreadful drivers about; the 'drive anything' sort, wheel groove cutters with steam plough rope or threshing belt, as the case might be. They had always lost or flogged their spanners, except perhaps a useless heavy one used for cracking coal instead of a hammer. They never wired their spud keys in, and they either had too much steam or not enough. Their smokeboxes were milky with prime and chimneys rusted, particularly a third of the way up at the rear where the regulator gland blew. The crank-shaft bearings would be saturated in oil and big ends flinging it everywhere; whilst links and crosshead would chatter, groan and thump in an agony of dryness. Golden dust from unoiled intermediate shaft bearings would shine like the Milky Way against a black night of sooty hornplates. The back axle lubricators would be running over with water from dripping water glasses, but not even this ever seeped through the long blocked feed pipes. Gears seen would be thick with cylinder oil, gears unseen as bright as silver.

Happily such were not the rule and an exemplar of the best type of driver is Art Pethick who drove a Robey road locomotive for S & T Trounson Ltd, of Redruth, Cornwall, before the 1914 war. John Trounson described one of his exploits:

During a severe winter when the roads were ice-bound there was an urgent need to deliver groceries to village shops in the high moorland country south of Redruth, but neither the firm's Fodens nor horse wagons could be used as the roads were in such a treacherous state. My father asked the resourceful Art whether he thought he could do the job with the Robey if she were only pulling a single truck and, as Arthur was prepared to try anything once, they set off on a bitterly cold Saturday morning when it was snowing occasionally as well as freezing. Under these conditions a fourth man was taken in case of emergencies. All went well until the evening when the engine slid into the hedge and it proved impossible to get her back on the road – and there she had to stay. It was bitterly cold and snowing at times, but fortunately there was a telephone close at hand and the crew were able to inform Head Office of their predicament.

I can see my father now, organising aid for the stranded men. He took with him all the rugs and blankets that we could produce at home, plus hot coffee in plenty and set off in a horse-drawn vehicle with the horses' hooves wrapped in sacking. Somehow, they reached the stranded engine and my father's advice to the men was to take plenty of sugar with the coffee and he told them that they could help themselves to any of the groceries and the firm would make it right with the shopkeepers. That night the four men huddled together on the footplate for warmth and, though steam was kept up, any drops of water from the injectors, etc. froze to form stalagmites on the road.

With dawn, the sun fortunately appeared and during the Sunday morning the thaw made it possible to get going again. The next to the last stop was made at the country pub at Wendron and there the crew 'warmed' themselves to such good effect that the return journey to Redruth was made in high style with the engine being belted along and throwing sparks galore! The final stop, not far from Wendron, was to deliver goods to another grocer but he was

Character in every line – the profile of Charles Theophilus Joyce who drove rollers for Eddison from 1905 to 1955 and part-time until 1958. He is now living near Chard in Somerset in his late eighties

Mr and Mrs Tom House in their living van in the days before Tom's retirement from driving steam rollers for the Eddison Steam Rolling Co of Fordington, Dorchester

Jack Herbert's 'Majestic' in the ditch near Charminster. The damage was, in fact, very slight

An Aveling & Porter single cylinder road locomotive owned by Thomas Wood & Sons of Crockenhill, Kent, not dated but c 1895

attending the evening service at the local Methodist chapel. That did not deter one of the distinctly 'merry' members of the crew from going to the chapel to call out the grocer to receive his supplies.

My own most vivid memory of boyhood engines at work in our own village is of an incident that happened about forty years ago when the county council were realigning the downhill double bend at the entrance to the village. Two rollers were used on the job and the smaller had the misfortune to back one rear wheel off the tarmacadam and into the soft verge of the village green which had been newly raised with soft earth to match the higher level of the new road surface. All efforts to extricate it failed. Plainly it was beyond the unaided efforts of the distressed roller, nor did it avail to bring the other roller round to the front to help through the medium of a good chain which had been conjured up and arranged round the forecarriage head of the embedded roller.

It was autumn, the afternoon was advancing and darkness was not far away. Since the problem could not be solved with what was to hand, outside help had to be sent for and the ganger accordingly disappeared into the phone box. We stood around speculating on what form the help would take. We did not have long to wait, for a quarter of an hour or so later we heard the unmistakeable sound of one of the Foden steam wagons pounding, with considerable haste, along the straight from the Home Farm and up the hill past the Long Pond. Half a minute later there was the characteristic 'Pom Pom Pom' in the chimney as the driver eased off the steam and the wagon coasted into view to draw up simmering with latent power at the downcast group by the horse-trough. There was a pause for a brief conference. I cannot recall who was driving the wagon. It may have been Bill Sedgwick but I cannot be sure. The plan of campaign settled, he climbed in again, ran along to the school, turned, came back and stationed himself in front of the second roller.

The excitement was tense. A knot of sightseers had gathered, people were standing at cottage doors and the doors of the shops. The policeman emerged from his house and warned us all to keep back. It was getting dark and the mate lit the lamps on the wagon. Meanwhile a second stout chain and shackle had been produced and the wagon coupled to the second roller. Providentially or thoughtfully the wagon had several tons of stone on board which served as ballast. Some of the men had dug out the ground in front of the ditched wheel of the roller to help form a ramp. Gingerly the wagon edged forward until all the chains were in tension.

In a minute or two all was ready. The policeman stopped the traffic, the mate climbed up into the wagon and, at a signal from the ganger all three drivers opened up their engines. The noise was terrific. The wheels of the rollers were spinning and grating on the road and their exhausts were shooting sparks high out of the chimneys. The wagon was on double-high and gave one or two thunderous exhaust beats, followed by a series of rapid urgent blasts as it mastered the load and the sunken wheel came up on to the hard road. There was a shout 'She's out'. It would have needed very little to make the onlookers cheer.

5. The Outsiders

The owners of engines used for threshing soon found there was work for them to be doing, out of the threshing season, in general haulage. Distributing roadstone, by contract, for the various road authorities was a mainstay of this out of season work for the stone was moved out during the summer to roadside depots where it was broken by the stone cracker and spread on the roads from a horse and cart or a hand-barrow during the winter. Quarry-owners were often farmers as well, in those days of small undertakings, and soon the trades of traction engine owner, haulage contractor, farmer, threshing contractor and quarry owner were nicely linked and cross linked by family ties. The road-stone business expanded a lot when rural road improvement began to gain real impetus during the closing decade of the last century. About that time steam rolling was gradually introduced on country roads and provided another area into which the village engine owner could expand. Rural district councils, who all had road making duties, were small and impecunious. Often they were understandably reluctant to embark on the purchase of a steam roller and preferred to hire one, a need which a good number

About the turn of the century driver Jock Dell posed for this photograph with the Oxford Steam Plough Co's No 1 roller (Fowler No 7164 of 1894) whilst rolling waterbound macadam for Bucks County Council not far from Buckingham, attended by a horse-drawn water cart for wetting the roadstone and men with brooms for brushing in the binder

In the summer of 1925 Thornbury (Gloucestershire) RDC's No 3 wagon – a Garrett – waits with the grit that is to cover the tar about to be applied by the horse-drawn and hand-pumped sprayer in the background

of threshing or ploughing contractors stepped in to fill.

County councils, who managed the main roads – roughly the present classified roads – were divided on the issue of roller ownership. Some, like Nottinghamshire, whose engineer, E. Purnell Hooley, was the inventor of tarmac, were early into ownership and had a substantial fleet of rollers by the mid-nineties. Gloucestershire was another county well in the van of ownership. My own home county of Kent had Henry Maybury as its engineer. He held back for another ten years but, having embarked upon the policy of ownership, the council went into it whole-heartedly by not only doing their own steam rolling but also setting up a fleet of steam tractors and trucks to carry out stone carting. With good local patriotism they bought their engines from Aveling & Porter Ltd whose works was at Rochester, Kent but the change to direct labour ruined a number of local contractors, including Jesse Ellis of Maidstone.

However, stone carting, though important, was not the only source of revenue to the engine owners and a good deal of general carting was done, often to and from the nearest railway station, for Victorian village traffic was railborne to an extent which we would find difficult to envisage. Bricks, building sand, lime, chalk, cement, grain, flour and manure were among the loads conveyed locally by traction engines. The late Chris Lambert of Horsmonden, and his father William before him, had a regular traffic in stable manure between the local stations and the hop farms of the district. The horses which drew London's traffic provided the manure and the voracious hop bines the crop which consumed it. Night soil from towns with no sewers was a noisome but considerable traffic in the early days. It was while a young man named Moses Martin was driving one of Jesse Ellis's Aveling & Porter engines through Maidstone one night in December 1880 on this duty that it blew up, probably because he, or a workmate, had screwed down the safety valve to an excessive pressure. This traffic in ordure declined as main sewers increased. The explosion, by the way, was referred to in Maidstone for years afterwards as the greatest on earth – it had shaken All Saints and rocked 'The Globe'.

Here and there in the seventies and eighties specialised steam haulage firms grew up, devoting all their energies to the carriage of goods. Such a one was the Cheadle Carrying Co in Staffordshire, owners of the famous Fowler 'Progress,' one of the few conventional traction engines built on three wheels. The single leading wheel made it, however, somewhat difficult to steer and what enginemen called 'light on'. That is to say being lighter at the front end than a conventional four-wheeled engine it had a tendency to rear up at the front when starting under load. Such concerns as the Cheadle Carrying Co were relatively rare, however, in the country-side and most of the firms venturing into heavy haulage by steam belonged to the large cities. So great, indeed, were the legislative disabilities on heavy haulage engines and so poor the general state of country roads that it was largely a short distance town trade until the 1896 Act relieved road traffic of some of its grosser disabilities.

One of the more memorable feats of long distance steam haulage of the earlier years of this century was the haulage of the large block of granite which formed the pedestal of the statue of King Alfred in Winchester from Penryn quarry in Cornwall. This was accomplished by a pair of Fowler engines belonging to John Freeman & McLeod Ltd who also owned the quarry. The piece of granite weighed 40 tons and it must have produced considerable excitement in the villages along the way.

Villages near the quarries, however, became blasé about the engines. The folk who lived in Easton and Church Hope, in the Isle of Portland, also, thought little of the feats of haulage performed on the hilly roads of the island by the road locomotives used in the quarries despite the fact that to take an engine and loaded trucks down the precipitous road to the causeway leading to Weymouth and the mainland, with the hairpin bend in the middle of the hill, was, looked at in cold blood, a job for heroes. To have failed to take the hairpin would have sent engine and crew several hundred feet down an almost sheer face on to rocks below. Familiarity, as ever, bred contempt, however, both in the beholders and the beheld and probably the effect of the once-in-a-lifetime sight of some of Norman Box's fleet of Fowlers with a huge out-of-gauge load, through a quiet country place, left a more indelible record on the memories of those who saw it than was left by the feats of skill performed many times each week by the drivers on Portland.

One of the largest indivisible loads ever moved upon the road by steam was a steam accumulator transported by Pickfords, who had taken over the Norman Box firm. The steam accumulator was moved 325 miles from Cochrane's boiler works at Annan, in Dumfriesshire, to the Gas Light & Coke Company's works at Beckton in East London. The journey began on 6 January 1938 and lasted three weeks though only eighteen days were spent actually on the move, averaging about 2 mph for the whole trip, which included struggling through snow over Shap Summit in Cumberland. The last lap through London was accomplished at night in fine style, through cleared streets, at an average of 3 mph. For the job Pickfords used two of the big Fowler road locomotives built for Norman Box, named 'Talisman' and 'Ajax' with a similar, but smaller, engine 'Jix' hauling the living wagon in which the crews ate and slept and providing help at the rear of the load when needed. The haul was mostly on the Great North Road, where, by this time, heavy traffic had ceased to amaze the inhabitants of the local villages.

The same could not be said of the feats of haulage accomplished in Scotland in moving machinery to the hydro-electric schemes set up in the thirties. Kerrs of Mavisbank, Glasgow were probably the most experienced hauliers in Scotland at the time. Because most of their trade had been with the shipyards and railway locomotive builders of Glasgow who were both, in the midst of the depression, desperately short of work, Kerrs were in sore straits, but the hydro-electric schemes, in true bureaucratic fashion, were administered from Edinburgh and the firms invited to tender for haulage were based in England. As Tom McTaggart of Kerrs remarked to me 'I doot they'd haird o' Glasgow.' The successful tenderers were Coulsons of Park Royal, London, whose first task was to transfer their equipment from London the four hundred or so miles to the loading point. They did not have a happy time on the contract. Their men, being Londoners, had trouble with the Scottish accents of the local folk, and vice versa, and the lightly built roads over peaty subsoils which the loads had to traverse in the Tummel area caused them infinite problems, the wheels often bursting down through the frail crust so that they ended up by 'plating' virtually the whole way, that is to say interposing slabs of steel plate between each wheel and the road, lifting the plates after the wheels had passed over them, moving them forward and putting them down again in front. Plating was laborious and monotonous to an unbelievable degree and, because of their early troubles, Coulsons probably did more of it than they need have done on the latter part of the journey because of their lack of local knowledge. It took them three weeks to cover five miles, a sight not seen in those villages, or anywhere else, since.

These troubles did not go unnoticed at Mavisbank and when the next contract came up for tender Robert Kerr saw to it that his firm was invited to bid – by lobbying the directors of the Grampian Hydro-Electric board in Edinburgh – and, moreover, that their tender was keen enough to secure them the contract. They hauled several thirty and forty ton transformers in 1933 using multi-wheeled trailers on solid rubber tyres whilst their competitors were still using antiquated

Coulsons Fowler No 9904 (MT 2430) near Rannoch Station in 1930 with another Fowler hired in Scotland from W. Adamson of Errol. Notice how the engines are scotched up. Coulson's engine (with the cab) is hauling the load with its wire rope. The leading engine is anchor-man. The steel plates used under the wheels to spread the load can be seen in front of the leading trolley

Roadside replacement of the broken rear axle of a Garrett No 6 Road Locomotive. The lost rear wheel is standing under the sheer legs on the left with a pole through the centre for handling purposes. The man with the chain is Jack Newstead and the tall man on his left Tom Staulkey, both from Garretts works. The man second from the left is a works labourer named Cook. These activities took up most of the road but pre 1914 no one seemed to mind

A timber-loading scene of the mid-twenties. Playle Bros' (of Maldon, Essex) Garrett tractor (No 34021) rolling up a large oak trunk. Note how skilful positioning of the rolling chains is taking it up evenly and the very strong timber tug. Many timber hauliers made do with much inferior equipment

heavy haulier's bogies on solid cast iron wheels. Soon afterwards they moved a seventy-five ton transformer from Abernethy to Newburgh, about five miles in three hours. Coulsons would have taken three weeks, completely obstructing the road so that the buses would have had to run up to each side of the obstruction and the passengers walk past it.

The feats performed by the heavy hauliers were not only prodigious in their accomplishments but also in the modesty of the equipment with which the deeds were done: steel plates to put down on the road, some good jacks (but rarely anything as modern as a hydraulic jack), plenty of chains and shackles, the wire ropes on the engines, scotches and timber packing. Beyond this the operations relied upon the power of the engines and the collective experience of the men who manned them. In works to dock haulage in a big city loads were usually craned on and off the trucks, but when it came to delivering a big machine to a works in a more rural situation things were different. Kerrs once delivered the anvil block of a stamping machine in three pieces, weighing respectively 119 tons, 99 tons and 90 tons from Auchincruive Station to the Ayr Stampworks Ltd. It was roped into the building on rails and placed on timber packing over the pit where it was to rest and was then lowered into position. Using only jacks and the power of their muscles, James Barnes and an outdoor erection gang spent six weeks on the job, quietly jacking and removing packing piece by piece 3in at a time until the press was in its final position in the pit.

Moving a heavy load round an otherwise impossibly sharp corner was accomplished by putting down plates under the wheels, wetting them or putting soft-soap on them and moving the trolley bodily sideways by pushing or pulling with an engine. The villages which saw this type of activity were, on the whole, either in industrial areas or along main roads. Rural haulage was rather different but not without its problems. Indeed in some ways it was more exacting. Eighteen months of surveys, planning and arranging had preceded the journey of 'Talisman' and 'Ajax' from Annan to Beckton and the crews had a back-up organisation to rely upon. The average haulier's men had only their own initiative to get them through. This is clearly shown in Mr J. Aldrich's account of an adventure timber hauling near Norwich:

I had three elms on a drug sixty-three feet long, from Woodton Old Hall; they weighed eleven tons, and were loaded with a Clayton crane engine. After they were loaded, I asked Jack (the driver of the crane engine) to help me pull them out to the road, as I had only a Garrett No 4 tractor and I had to come out between two ponds, but he wouldn't. So I got plenty of steam, and she pulled them all right until I got to the ponds, where it was a bit uphill; so I took the tractor off, and I had two 15ft chains with which I chained the front of the tractor to a tree on a bank, and blocked the back. When I pulled the rope broke, so I tied a knot in it but that didn't hold, so I had to splice it. I just don't know how she shifted it but she did, and it was eight o'clock at night before I got on to the road; so I decided to leave the drug at the 'Dick' public house, and stop in the van for the night. When I pulled in the pub yard, I swept the hedge down!

The next morning I got on the road for Norwich City station, and they were steam rolling just through Woodton and the tractor scrabbed herself in on the road. I asked the driver of the steam roller to help me out, but he said he was afraid he would pull the tank off. So I ran the tractor forward, blocked her and put a chain from the pin to the back wheel, and roped the load again, which brought the comment from the roller driver, 'You've got a good bit of stuff there.' As I turned into the station yard at Norwich, I was told by my partner that the trees only missed the windows by inches.

Timber hauling was a job for the man who knew what he was doing. The engine did not, in general, have much to do with getting the tree down except where it had an awkward lean that made it menace a building or a road or be likely to fall into a river or on an adjoining owner's land. Here a pull from the wire rope might be needed but as a general rule it was not. What the engine did have to do, however, was to snig the timber out of the wood to a point where it could be loaded, load it on to the timber tug (in Kent and Sussex) or 'drug' (East Anglia), get the loaded tug on to the road and haul it to the mill or railway station – which could be no small task as Mr Aldrich's account shows. He was fortunate in that his task began after the timber was loaded. He, and his mate, might have had to load it as well. Loading was done with a rolling rope. The tree trunk was drawn alongside the tug and about six to eight feet distant from it. The engine positioned itself on the other side of the tug and the wire rope was run out over the tug, and hooked to two rolling chains over the trunk, which returned under the trunk and were anchored to opposite ends of the tug. Two hardwood

A corner of the works yard of Jesse Ellis & Co at Maidstone, c 1893. Jesse himself poses in front of an Aveling & Porter high wheeled road engine and the man on the footplate of the engine is reputed to be the celebrated Tom Boarer who had only one hand but still contrived to manage an engine

The scene in Main Street, Otterburn, (Northumberland) during road works in 1914. The steam wagons were Fodens and belonged to Northumberland County Council as did the Aveling & Porter roller (No 4551) 'Lord Roberts' in the centre. The two road locomotives were Fowlers (Nos 8290 and 11066) owned by Wear Bros of Hexham. Of all those in the picture the only one still alive is Gladys Corbett, the girl on the extreme right. Foden No 8 (works No 4368) was new that year and doubtless George Oliver (resting on its front wheel) was very proud of it. Bob Rutherford (fifth man from the right) drove one of the other Fodens and lived round the corner to the left. The building on the left is part of the Murray Arms (now the Percy Arms). The shop behind wagon No 8 was kept by a Miss Douglas known to the locals as 'Old Meg'

skids squared at the ends were fitted into sockets on the cross bolsters of the tug to form ramps and as the engine began to wind in the rope the tree would roll forward, up the ramps and on to the tug, provided, of course, – and here the skill came in – that the chains were placed so as to catch the tree at the point of balance of the trunk. Skill on the part of the driver was very necessary but the loader, the second man, was the key to successful loading, a point which the late P. A. Mathieson, whom we have met before giving an account of thresher followers, made amusingly when setting down an account of a typical day when he was himself a loader:

Now we will fetch a load in; a typical day, loading oak. We have a Foster five ton two-speed gear-drive steam tractor, and a timber wagon; both (of course) with steel tyres all round. The usual radius from the sawmills was about fifteen–twenty miles.

On arrival at the felled timber (either coppice or hedgerow), it was always the same. The 'fust' job was to have a look at it, while the driver weighs up how to get in; later he will wonder how to get out. The loader (and, incidentally, I never did own up to being a driver's mate); not that I have anything against steam engine drivers, they were nearly all good, only I was unlucky in that I never worked with a good 'un. The loader, then, selects the loading site and instructs the driver where to set the engine. Note here how the loader suddenly takes charge.

This sends the driver on a long detour, and he seems to take half a mile to turn round in. The loader looks the sticks over, and selects one bearing the mystic signs, scribed or chalked, 10; 43 × 18.1. When translated, this means tree No 10, 43ft long, 18$\frac{1}{4}$in quarter girth. The loader knows what's in a stick by just looking at it (with a sly peep at the Hoppus measurer), and he works it out at nearly 'a undurd fut'. To be exact, it is 99ft 6in, and that's b— near 100ft anyhow!

The loader now looks round for his wagon. The driver is just bringing her in, and the upraised arm of the loader tells him where to stop. The driver at this stage of the proceedings apparently becomes stone-deaf; it is no use shouting; you must give him the sign. With the wagon well set, the loader unhooks the pin from the drawbar, and the skids are now put into position. While this heavy task is performed by the loader, the driver is hard on at some job drivers have to do; stoking, oiling (even transferring a rabbit from coal bunker to dinner basket), or some queer job that only a driver would think of!

When he's ready, the driver sets the 'little owd Foster' for a dead straight wind. That there is sixty yards of rope on the winding drum and it is fifty-nine yards to the stick is smart work on his part; it does not concern him at all that the loader has to pull the rope out. At the end of a desperate struggle, the loader finds that he has to go back to the 'injun' to fetch a chain. He then discovers that he cannot get the chain under the stick, so he goes to the wagon to fetch an iron bar with which to grub under the stick. An extensive search fails to reveal any bar, so he consults the driver. 'It were on when we started, must have fell off' (which it had). In blaming the driver for this, the fact that he (the loader) was riding on the wagon when the bar fell off, and should have seen it, does not occur to him!

At all events, he goes back to the stick and digs furiously underneath it with a piece of wood. He fixes the chain round, then realises he must go back to the wagon yet again to fetch a C hook, so as to couple the chain to the wire rope.

We now come to where the loader gets his own back on the driver. His upraised arm means *pull*; it is no use shouting, and we have not got a team of timber 'hosses' anyway. So the driver starts to wind, and his anxious look means that he does not know whether the 'owd gel' can do it. The stick moves slowly, then jams against a stump. This causes the Foster to sit back with her front wheels reared in the air. The loader, having had his joke, proceeds to give the stick a half-roll. When translated from timber haulier's jargon, this means turning the chain round the stick so that when the engine winds it turns the stick half over. The loader should have done this in the first place.

Garrett 4 ton steam wagon No 34404 (24th November 1923) used by the Haslemere UDC as a maid of all work. Here it is being used as a refuse collector. It also had a sludge tank body for emptying cesspools and was further used as a tipping lorry on roadwork.

Some nifty work by the driver (notice how loaders give the driver the credit) brings the stick up to the base of the skids. The loader gauges the distance to the bolsters and, having got this to his liking, proceeds to deftly place the rolling chains in position. The driver sets the Foster on the other side of the wagon for a dead straight wind. Meanwhile, the loader cusses about that missing bar; but having got the chains nicely adjusted he gives the driver the sign.

There are now some tense moments while the stick rolls slowly up the skids; but it drops fair and square on the bolsters, and is well and truly loaded. Another stick is wound in (it's no good trying to tush today), and this too is deftly loaded. This one is marked 7; 38 × 20.2, being tree No 7, 38ft long, $20\frac{1}{2}$in quarter girth, which is equal to 110 cu ft 10 in. It is thus a larger stick than the first, but it fits well into the bed. The driver wonders what size stick the loader is going to top up with, and suggests a fifty-footer; but the loader is intent on another 'undurd fut'. Three good sticks is a tidy load of about 310 'fut', and with about 25 'fut' to the ton it weighs about 12 tons.

The next job is to chain the load on before attempting to move off. The front bolster first; hook on, sling the chain over, hook on the other side.

Thomas Wood & Sons bought this Sentinel six-wheeled steam waggon (No 7953) (Sentinel always spelled it that way) in July 1929 and whilst it was brand new had this picture taken of it whilst being loaded with flints in Knatts Valley, a fold of the Downs a few miles from their works.

Now comes the wresting; with an ash pole inserted under the chain, pulled round and down and secured. The same with the rear bolster.

All hell is let loose roping the load out. The driver blames the loader (of course); 'shouldn't have put so much on.' Out on the road at last, with spuds off and lamps lighted, as of course by this time it is pitch dark. But all's well, we stop at a pub; and it was always a loaded timber wagon pulled up at the pub.

As Edwin Forth related on another occasion it was, indeed, a rare thing for an old time engine driver to be able to pass a congenial pub when he had the price of a pint in his pocket – unless, of course, he was, like the late Jack Richards one of the select band of teetotal drivers.

Hauling timber by tractor one could get the whole of the weight which the engine was capable of hauling upon a single wagon or tug, but a bigger engine, such as the Clayton & Shuttleworth road locomotive owned and worked by Charles Miles, the Sawmiller from Stamford, Lincolnshire, usually managed two wagons which were proportionately more difficult to manage on the road. Miles' engine was driven by a character known as 'Pincher', a great beer drinker who, nevertheless, was never to be seen on the engine the worse for drink. Pincher, as far as is known, had no home and no possessions beyond his apparel. He slept wrapped in a tarpaulin under the engine, a rough, dirty old man who was a super-lative performer at his trade.

Tom Newell and his sons Jack and Bill, carried on a timber haulage business by steam at Westerham, Kent, in the twenties and thirties. Tom had had varied experience in road haulage, including some years of driving for Lalonde Bros & Parham of Weston-super-Mare on furniture work. He could do wonders in getting work out of an engine which, as a matter of habit, he drove pretty hard. His social drawback was his bitterly sarcastic tongue with which he used to lash all those who worked with him into greater effort. He had, however, lived and worked in hard times and, in his turn, had suffered in the same way from older men so probably could see no reason why the succeeding generation should escape what he had had to put up with. It is perhaps arguable that to be cantankerous and perverse is the traditional revenge of the old for the loss of their youth. In Tom's day living conditions were that much harder and men aged more prematurely which may go some way to accounting for the undeniable fact that many senior members of the engine-driving fraternity were capable of being crotchety in the extreme. In their defence it must be said that the owner of an engine invariably laid the whole responsibility for the way it was utilised upon the driver and it is under-standable that he (the driver) was irritated by any shortcomings in the work of the men under him when he knew that the blame would fall upon him.

It was an observable phenomenon that drivers employed by public bodies or by companies sufficiently well-to-do to afford to be more tolerant were themselves less harsh with their mates. The men who drove for the brewery or the Council had a rather smaller share, on the whole, of the habits which made their confreres on threshing or timber-hauling so difficult to work with. That is not to say they were never at odds with their mates but the atmosphere tended more to geniality. Brewing, in any case, tended, at the turn of the century, to be much more of a local affair. Of course, there were the famous national names like Bass and Guinness but a great deal of the beer consumed in villages was locally made, possibly even in the village itself. Some charming village breweries survived into quite recent times – Garne's at Burford in Oxfordshire and Phillips at Downham Market in Norfolk are two that come to mind – but attrition was a continuous process and amalgamations and the tied house system had swept many away long before my time. Within the lives of my father and father-in-law, however, in the district within fifteen miles of Tonbridge there were twelve breweries. In the town itself there was Bartrups; at Tunbridge Wells Kelseys, in Sevenoaks two – Goldings and Blighs. There were the Black Eagle Brewery at Westerham, Wares at Frant, Kenward & Court (for whom my father-in-law worked) at Hadlow, Wickhams at Yalding, Smiths at Lamberhurst and Phillips at Malling. At the village of Wateringbury two breweries flourished – Leneys and Jude Hanbury, whilst Goldings had a second brewery at Wrotham. It did not stop there, either, for

Always pioneers, Thomas Wood & Sons of Crockenhill, Kent, bought the Foden steam wagon, No 538, with high rear wheels and outside frame, new in 1902. The picture shows it collecting apple baskets lettered in its owner's name from Swanley Basket Works

The late John Hardy of Blackmore, Essex owned two Burrell rollers named *Florence* and *Lorna*. This is one of them working on the resurfacing of Widford Road, Ingatestone, Essex in the thirties. The man with the water can standing by the roller is keeping the wheels wet to avoid the bituminous road metal adhering to them.

other brewers, from outside the district, came in to supply pubs which they had bought.

Steam power was used for pumps and for driving machines in most of these breweries and brewers, as a race, believed in its use. On the other hand, many deliveries were very local and, whilst the traction engine, a relatively large machine, remained the standard motive power for steam haulage on the road, it was often just as convenient to have the fetching in of coal, barley, stout and sugar done by a local engine owner as to have a traction engine actually on the brewery strength, though some brewers did especially if they had houses further afield, enabling the engine to be used for what otherwise would have meant a long haul for horses or sending the beer by train. Steam haulage became attractive to brewers when the lighter and faster steam tractors and steam wagons became available, namely in the first decade of this century. Brewers with the greatest distances to cover – which meant, on the whole, those in the larger way of business – took up steam transport with the greatest enthusiasm. To my knowledge, of the brewers in my list, Kelseys, Kenward & Court, Smiths and Leneys had steam wagons. Smiths had, at one time, an old wagon built by the firm of Wallis & Steevens Ltd at Basingstoke. These were never a nimble breed, even on level ground, and the brewery lay in a valley, approached in either direction by steep hills which were a grievous trial to the wagon. It was rare to see a brewery steam wagon in anything but tip-top condition and the drivers and mates, accoutred in the leather aprons of their calling, had an air of prosperity and well being, aided no doubt by a characteristically prodigious consumption of beer. One drayman of Kelseys reckoned to have a gallon before breakfast and it was the custom of the publicans to give both driver and trouncer a pint when they had completed a delivery so that their total daily consumption must have been considerable. Brewery transport, whether horse, steam or motor, was traditionally driven with great rectitude possibly because the drivers realised that they would, having taken a fair amount of ale, be in danger of having ascribed to them the blame, whether deserved or not, for any accident in which they might have the misfortune to become involved.

Millers too found steam useful and stuck to it for a long time. A miller's wagon, in fact, owned by Kingsford & Co of Barton near Canterbury, was the last steam wagon to trade into our village. I left the village finally in 1949 and it continued for a year or two after that. The wagon was not built until the mid-thirties, was fast and modern and, hence, much admired. It used to draw a trailer as far as the village bakery when the last of the trailer's load would be discharged. Leaving the trailer in the village it would go on solo doing a loop, during the afternoon, through the villages to Edenbridge and back, picking up the trailer about teatime and setting off on the fifty mile trek back to Canterbury.

We also used to enjoy the visits of the steam wagons and rollers of the County Council and, a little earlier, the steam tractors and trailers of the Sevenoaks Rural District Council. Our house stood next to the 'Bat & Ball' public house in the village street and on the other side of the pub was the general shop kept by 'Chicky' (William) Sherman. He opened early and closed late and his shop

Driver Samways pauses for the photographer with the roadmen and Eddison's number 100 (Aveling & Porter No 4919 of 1901). c 1914

The 'little owd Foster' – a scene at Woodborough (Notts) in 1922 from the camera of the late Fred Gillford showing a Foster five ton compound tractor (No 14349 of 1914). Note the wresting bat keeping tight the chain round the tree trunk on the timber carriage and the traditional wheelwrights wheels on the timber tug with their wooden naves

When Charles Marston, the Bungay miller, wanted a steam wagon in 1912 it was no surprise that he chose one made about twenty miles away by Garretts of Leiston (Works No 30826) but economically he used up one of his horse-drawn vans as a trailer. Note the smartly polished acetylene head lamp

and the 'Bat' were the reasons for many a stop by the wagons and tractors either for beer or tobacco. He used to sell loose tobacco from large tin canisters, weighing it out by the ounce on a pair of scales used for nothing else and tipping it direct from the brass scale pan into the buyer's tobacco pouch. The county council Foden steam wagons were used on rough work but always ran well and the drivers kept them very clean, never failing to turn them out with the brass bright. I have very happy memories of these wagons pausing outside our house, their loads of tarmac fragrant with hot coal tar, the pop and sizzle of a bead of water and oil dropping on to the hot wrapper plates of the firebox and then, as they moved off, the abrupt cough of the first exhaust beat and the urgent lift and surge forward as the slight slack took up in the driving chain.

It was made more interesting still by the fact that the drivers were mostly local men whom we knew by name. A recall of the names shows the popularity of the Christian name 'William' with the parents of that generation. There was Bill ('Fat-eye') Sedgwick who drove, first a steam tractor and subsequently a steam wagon, Bill Marchant who drove the RDC roller, Bill Pope, who drove for the county council, Nobby Mustill, who worked for the neighbouring Tonbridge RDC, Len Rolf, another county council driver and Bob Hatch, a kindly soul but indifferent driver who had various employers.

Not all council vehicles were engaged upon the haulage of road materials, however, and other, less salubrious, duties came their way. Haslemere council, in the south of Surrey, had a Garrett undertype steam wagon which was particularly versatile. Equipped with a tank body it emptied cesspools. By an exchange of bodies it became a refuse collector and by a third metamorphosis it was adapted for carrying road-stone. I do not recall anything similar being used locally. Our own village of Leigh, thanks to the improvements made by the first Lord Hollanden, was sewered but where there were no sewers what may euphemistically be called 'other means' of disposal were used, which might equate to a tank cart, to a conveniently leaky cesspool or to a bucket for solids and a nearby ditch for waste water except, of course, that there was much less waste water for, with no piped supplies, one tended to be very sparing with what had to be pumped by hand or drawn up in a bucket and, in the summer, what waste there was was snapped up for watering the garden. Cesspool emptiers and gully emptiers were, in short, mainly for the environs of towns and penetrated into the deep country mostly in the motor era and after steam had ceased to be used.

Mines, cement or brickworks, sand and gravel pits, and quarries were also numbered amongst village steam users, whilst paper mills and spinning mills, often in village situations also favoured steam. In the Lancashire cotton belt owners of village cotton mills took to steam wagons, either their own or those of hauliers, as a supplement to or substitute for, railway cartage. In Kent we had paper mills but no spinning mills. When I was a schoolboy the paper mill at Roughway, a few miles north of Tonbridge used to have a very aged Sentinel steam wagon with which forays to the Tonbridge railway yard were made to collect coal.

Mr & Mrs William Henry Bennion, host and hostess of the New Inn, Blackheath (Warks) pose on either side of the driver of the City Brewery Co (Lichfield) Ltd's Garrett wagon (works No 31631). The trouncer is seated behind the driver. The costume suggests about 1914 but no definite date is known

On the return trip the old wagon would plod wearily the whole length of the High Street and up the rise of Dry Hill. Naughty boys on bikes would hang on to the ironwork of the tail board for a pull up the hill, a dangerous pastime which irked the crew, and the mate used to lean far out of the cab hurling lurid invective and small pieces of coke at the miscreants.

Until the recession of the thirties stifled Cornish tin and copper mining the mines of Cornwall sustained some interesting steam transport and some highly original characters who drove them but trades other than mining in Cornwall also harboured steam engine drivers somewhat out of the ordinary run of men. My friend Jack Trounson (b 1905) was not only born and brought up in Cornwall but worked there as a mining engineer throughout his working life. Consequently he knew many of these Cornish worthies. One of those he recalled was the late Jack Richards, who drove a big Aveling & Porter engine for the Hayle firm of Hosken, Trevithick, Polkinghorne & Co Ltd, millers and corn merchants. Unlike many enginemen Jack Richards was teetotal and this is how John Trounson recalled him:

He was, I believe, a Methodist local preacher and his clothes were as clean as his engine, which was always immaculate. She was not the best of steamers but he certainly knew how to handle her. Admittedly, a two-speed Aveling is

An Aveling & Porter traction engine owned by William Lambert of Horsmonden, with three truckloads of bricks outside High Brooms Brickworks, near Tunbridge Wells, about the turn of the century.

not a high-geared engine, but it is said that he could go with three loaded trucks from Truro station to Hayle, about twenty miles over hilly ground, without ever changing from fast wheel.

The last big engine bought by HTP & Co was a new eight horse-power three-speed Fowler and the maker's man came down with her. As senior driver, Jack Richards was given the option of taking over the new engine but he preferred to retain his Aveling. Fowler's man challenged Jack that he could go from Penzance to Hayle, ie about nine miles of not very hilly ground, considerably faster than Jack could do with his Aveling, but Jack denied this. The two engines therefore left Penzance almost simultaneously to settle the argument. Jack Richards arrived in Hayle, shunted his trucks, put the engine away in her shed and went out in the road and stood up with his hands in his pockets before the Fowler appeared. Needless to say, Jack continued to drive the Aveling.'

John Trounson's father was a miller and owned various Foden steam wagons and a big traction engine built by the firm of Robey in Lincoln, a not over success-ful engine. She had, however, a very large tank capacity and could travel quite long distances without stopping for water, a trait which on at least one occasion stood her driver in very good stead. The engine was driven by John's friend

Arthur Pethick, one of the few men able to get satisfactory work out of the rather temperamental machine. Let John himself take up the story:

On this occasion a big grain ship was discharging her cargo at the port of Falmouth and numerous local tractions were engaged in working to and from the port. On his way up the steep hill at Ponsanooth, Art, on the Robey, was overtaken by a remarkable seven horse power single-crank compound Burrell, which was a most powerful old engine and one which was driven by a noted character, Jack King. The latter was a big man who wore a huge watch chain across an ample stomach, and when he overtook another engine he had a habit of holding out the chain as if to say 'Do you want a pull?'

This he did again that day and rushed ahead of the Robey, obviously bent on reaching the next water stop first. There was only room for one engine at a time at the said water pick-up and Jack King thought that if he could get there first he would be in Falmouth before the Robey and so get loaded first and be on his way homeward long before Art. The latter, realising what was afoot, made no attempt to overtake the Burrell, but when Jack King had stopped and lowered the hose the Robey suddenly appeared, going like the wind, and sailed past secure in the knowledge that they could reach Falmouth and get back to this spot before they had to refill their enormous tanks! Jack King was completely outwitted and could only shake his fist at the receding Robey.

Perhaps one of the most celebrated Cornish traction engine drivers was an adept but notoriously cantankerous character called Joe Beck who drove an Aveling & Porter crane engine, ie a traction engine with a fixed crane jib at the front end, for Harveys of Hayle Foundry. John Trounson said:

There is an entertaining story told about something which happened when the main beam of the pumping engine at the Levant mine broke. This mine is on the north coast at Pendeen, about six miles from the Land's End and the engine house, where the new beam had to be off-loaded, is almost on the edge of the high cliffs and approached by a steep and dangerous road.

Harvey's had made the new beam, which consisted of two castings, probably weighing six-seven tons apiece. Joe Beck arrived with these behind his crane engine, carefully sized up the situation and successfully took the engine and load down to where it had to be delivered. Not content with having done this, he remarked casually to the engineer of the mine, 'Shall I put 'em up for 'ee with the engine Mister?' The offer was declined with thanks as all the heavy lifting tackle had already been placed in position for the job.

A staple of the Cornish industrial economy was china clay mining, a good deal of the traffic of which was handled by industrial railways but in connection with

The Garrett steam wagon (No 30997) and some of the staff of Lumsden & Mackenzie at Stormontfield near Perth pose together at the gate of the bleaching works in 1913. The wagon was painted smoke grey and lettered in red. Finished in August 1912 for Muscate of Danzig it was returned by them and sold to Lumsden & Mackenzie the following March

which road engines were used as well. One of the stations used for transhipment to rail was Grampound Road. Until just after the 1914–18 war an engine owner named Keast had four big engines, built by Charles Burrell & Son Ltd of Thetford, Norfolk, engaged in this work and after he retired from business one of his drivers, Arthur Powell, bought the engine he had driven for many years, migrating with it to the Redruth area where he did a good deal of haulage with it for the mines. John Trounson said of this engine:

She was an engine with a long boiler and was officially named 'Martha', but unofficially 'Long-guts'. She must have been a fine machine in her time but when I knew her she was so badly run down as to appear a complete wreck. The chimney had been broken off and replaced by a much smaller bore parallel tube, the front wheels seemed to flap in the breeze as the bushes were so badly worn and the engine blew in every gland. Yet in spite of all appearances she was still very strong. Together with the East Pool mine six horse power Fowler, old 'Martha' transported a 48-ton pumping engine main beam from the Grenville to South Crofty mines in 1922, and in the following year the same two engines hauled a 52-ton engine beam from the Carn Brea mines to the then new shaft at East Pool. Together with the two very heavy trucks, the engines must then have been pulling well over 70 tons. Furthermore, part of the route lay over soft ground and it was necessary to lay heavy boiler plates beneath the wheels of the trucks in places. The weight was so great that the plates were being rolled into a curve again as if they were being put through bending rolls – I actually saw this – but the two engines were master of the job.

Such feats as this provided the villages through which the loads passed with topics for recall sufficient to last a lifetime but even the more mundane task of installing a new boiler in a country brewery made an entertaining spectacle for the inhabitants of Foxearth, in north Essex, in 1902. Ward & Sons' brewery, where the boiler was erected, brewed a very pleasant country beer of which I have consumed many enjoyable pints in a little pub that used to be theirs, opposite the railway station in Halstead, a few doors from Clover's flour mill. Now regrettably the station, the mill and the brewery firm exist only in memory but whilst all of them were still with us the late Gerald Dixon related the story of how the 'new' boiler was put in. He was working as an apprentice at the time for Barton & Co, a small firm of millwrights and engineers in Sudbury. This is how he described what to him, as a young apprentice, was a considerable adventure:

One afternoon the Governor, making his usual tour of inspection, said, 'Boy, go down to the Quay in the morning (for at that time the river was navigable from Sudbury to the sea) and steam the six-horse Aveling and bring her to the Works.'

I had left the engine at the Quay after a previous jaunt, and for me it was 'just what the doctor ordered', and I had not the slightest difficulty in turning out the following morning at the usual 5.45 am. I arrived at the works soon after 7 am wondering what was in store. The old boy was very soon in attendance and ordered me down to the nearby ditch to pick up water, then to draw the boiler trolley out into the lane running alongside the works, where several men were soon jacking up and oiling each wheel.

I was then told to go to breakfast, and hurry up, too, so off I went, thinking perhaps we might be going to move some heavy machinery, which on several special and notable occasions we had accomplished with the same tackle.

Breakfast over, I found coal heaped in the bunker and a steersman in attendance. Within a few minutes 'Jumbo' (that was our pet name for the governor) was driven out of the yard on the trade horse-drawn van, in turn loaded with snatch blocks, jacks, chains, etc. The order was 'Follow me', and he led us to Long Melford goods yard where, on two trucks, was loaded a Lancashire boiler, 32ft 6in by 8ft 6in – the largest I had ever seen. Of course, I then knew what we were after, but not our destination.

The late Gordon Smith of Hexham took this picture of his father's Foden wagon (No 5066) alongside an unidentified ex War Department Foden belonging to Northumberland County Council. H. F. Smith & Son were the third owners of No 5066. It was supplied new to H. & G. Dutfield Ltd, the London carriers, sold by them to Johnson Bros & Co, of Pickering in 1923 and purchased by Mr Smith in 1925

Two Garrett steam tractors, owned by Noah Etheridge of Blythborough (Suffolk) engaged upon brick cartage in Beccles about 1912

The transfer of the boiler from rail to trolley was very quickly accomplished by two railway cranes expertly handled. During this episode 'Jumbo' called me to one side and disclosed our destination, viz Foxearth Brewery; actually two and a half miles from the station by the normal route but, owing to the structure of the main bridge over the River Stour, we were to travel through Long Melford street to Glemsford, then to Pentlow and Foxearth. 'Mind what you get up to; now hook on to your load,' which I did, but could I get off? No; the Aveling just stood and scrapped.

It was obvious the engine was no good for the job, and the next order was 'Take it back to the yard and wait till I come.' This I did with the horrible feeling, that, as far as I was concerned, that was to be the end.

It was not long before 'Jumbo' put in an appearance; he eyed the engine and then turned his gaze on me, put both his hands in his trouser pockets, jingled his keys, rattled his money, hunched his shoulders and then said 'Go and steam the car (an 1899 Locomobile) and pick me up at the office.'

We were soon on our way to Belchamp, about five miles away, where in a field beside the road Joe Coe was threshing with his eight horse Robey of about 1875 vintage, which I had delivered and stayed with for a week's trials after a works rebuild the previous year. An animated conversation took place, 'Jumbo' returned to the car, and it was 'Home, John, and don't spare the horses.' An exchange of engines had been negotiated, so off once more with the Aveling and back into Sudbury with the Robey by 9 pm that evening; and with my tail up this time! Banked up, home, wash and feed, and so to bed.

Next morning we were again following the horse and van to Long Melford. The Robey raised no objections and we pulled out and started our journey without incident. I had been warned the old lady was due for a wash-out, and therefore had to use great caution, but as the route was nearly all rising ground we had no digestive troubles, although it was real collar work most of the time.

We picked up water three times during the journey of about eight miles. On arriving at the one and only bridge, 'Jumbo' alighted from the cart which had headed the procession, ordered everyone to stand clear and standing in the middle of the road, solemnly beckoned me on. The bridge held, normal relations were resumed, on we came, soon arriving at the foot of a long and very steep hill which was approached in low gear and showing a feather, but the Robey would have none of it and that is where the vanload of tackle came into the picture.

We had to make a number of short hauls with snatch block and double rope, chaining the engine hind wheels to front. At times on taking up the strain the Robey hopped like a great frog, and on the steepest gradient the whole outfit moved downhill instead of up.

All this took a long time, and we eventually arrived in Foxearth street well after 6 pm, and the whole village turned out to welcome us and watch the operation of turning in at an acute angle from a narrow country lane to the back entrance of the Brewery. Fortunately, this came off without damage to anything or anyone so, well, call it a day.

The next day found us winkling the load in a very restricted space in alignment with the prepared brickwork, using a snatch block and greased boiler plate.

It was this knack of carrying out work simply and thriftily which so characterised village life in the steam era. Nowadays there is a regrettable tendency to equate thrift with meanness. The mean man is never admirable and makes life poorer by begrudging the proper use of what he has, whereas the thrifty man makes it richer by getting more out of what is to hand. Years ago, when an oak tree was cut down not much was wasted. The trunk, as a matter of course, was cut up into scantlings for use in buildings or in framing up carts and wagons. The branches were used for firing or for distilling to charcoal, the twigs and small limbs were made into faggots for stack bottoms or for firing the brick oven, whilst the major limbs were sawn into gate posts or similar articles for use about the farm or estate. Quite often the trunk was barked so that the tanners might have the bark.

Conversion of round timber into scantlings was done traditionally over the saw pit, using a long double-handled pit saw, the top sawyer standing above the round timber and the bottom sawyer in a pit. Pit sawing required some skill but

Outside the Bear & Bells in the Old Market in Beccles, Suffolk a Garrett five ton steam wagon No 31226 owned by the Norfolk Motor Transport Co, paused for the photographer whilst delivering Whitbread's beer in 1913

it also entailed hour upon hour of sheer drudgery in uncomfortable conditions and it is not surprising therefore that sawyers acquired the reputation of drunkards or that sawing by steam power spread, in the second half of the last century, into most of the country sawmills to be found in the villages. Hand-sawing was slow to die. The 1914–18 war really finished off the last serious use of it but it was not until the village wheelwright and cartwright in his traditional form became extinct that the occasional use of the saw pit ceased. In my own lifetime, say forty-five years ago, I saw the saw pit in the village wheelwright's shop at Leigh used by 'Potty' Faircloth to rip down a large piece of squared timber for use in a wagon.

On the whole, however, sawing was done by steam *before* 1900. Pit sawyers had travelled from saw pit to saw pit, sawing out, by piecework, the timbers required by the builder, wheelwright or estate bailiff employing them because there was seldom enough work to keep them in one spot throughout the year. So, in the same way, steam sawing was often done by contract. Quite often, as on Lord Hollanden's estate at Leigh, the mill itself was static and only the men came round seasonally. It was always known in the village when they were coming by the fact that the estate portable steam engine, a Ransome, was taken from the Home Farm where it normally worked, through the length of the village to the Wood Lodge, as the sawmill was known.

An alternative to the method of the fixed sawmill and travelling sawyers was to employ a contractor who supplied both the men and the machines. The essential ingredients of such a travelling outfit were a rack saw-bench and an engine to drive it, usually with a cross cut saw as well to square off ends of sawn timber, to cut it to lengths and to cut up wane and offcuts to firewood lengths. Many of these latter were used to fire the engine. A rack-bench had a horizontal travelling table, long enough to take the piece of round timber which was being milled, mounted on rollers so that it could be propelled forward, either by hand, using a crank handle, or power, through a clutch and secondary belt, so as to advance the log progressively on to the saw. Such a rack-bench could handle timber up to about three feet in diameter, though many were smaller, but this was sufficient as prime butts were usually sold and the portable sawmills dealt with second grade stuff and tops and branches. Sometimes the sawyers lived in a caravan. Others slept rough in sheds or made themselves shelters on the site. It was a tough life and they had a reputation of taking their fun where they found it enjoying the beer and the girls and moving on before the consequences of any indiscretions became evident. Typically such a travelling outfit consisted of a traction engine for haulage, a portable for driving the bench, a living van, a truck, a timber tug and a water cart, but so plentiful were variations on this set-up that to generalise is a rash act. Sometime the traction engine powered the machinery, displacing the portable engine, but more often the function of the traction was to get the round timber to the mill site and haul away the sawn quarterings and boards either for local seasoning or to the railway station.

Reliance on rail transport at the turn of the century was more total than can

Allchin traction engine No 2146 driving a saw-bench in the village of Barrowden, Rutland in 1953. It was owned by Mr A. R. Storey. (*J. F. Clay*)

Only about fifteen miles from London, Sentinel steam waggon No 6400 owned and used by W. & J. Glossop Ltd as the power unit of a road burning plant, rests at Beddington Lane, Surrey in July 1971 in the long shadows of an evening sun. (*J. H. Meredith*)

The 48 ton cast iron beam of a 90in Cornish engine loaded on to trucks for transport from Grenville mine to South Crofty in 1922. The cylinder of the engine can be seen behind it. (*J. Trounson collection*)

The Grenville beam on the road to South Crofty. The leading engine is a 6 NHP Fowler owned by East Pool Mines and driven by Fred King but the second engine is the dilapidated but powerful 8 NHP Burrell 'Martha' (alias 'Long Guts') owned and driven by Art Powell. (*J. Trounson collection*)

106

now be grasped. For distances as short as eight or ten miles it was deemed worthwhile to load commodities on to the train and offload into carts again at the destination. Rail traffic, moreover, was handled briskly. In those days of non-refrigerated vans it had to be fast to handle perishable traffic. The revolution in the supply of fresh milk to London, which happened in the closing years of the nineteenth century, relied upon quick rail transport. Until that time London's milk came from cows kept and fed in mews and yards in the actual metropolis and the hay and straw on which these cows and the half million or so horses in London were fed and bedded was an important traffic.

The move away from town-kept cows was one of the ingredients of the agricultural revival of the nineties. The growth of the large dairy companies, public health legislation and public opinion, all played their parts in fanning out dairying for the London market into the home counties, but the quickness of the trains that ferried the milk into London each night made the operation possible. Transport from farm to station or farm to creamery was mostly by horse but by 1910 or so experiments were being made with collection by steam wagon. Cary & Grimsdell, for instance, who had a large dairy at Dorchester, bought a Garrett steam wagon in 1919 for use in collecting churned milk from Charminster and the dairy farms along the River Piddle whilst Atkins of Wool had a similar wagon for the same purpose in 1912. After the 1914–18 war road transport played a larger part in milk collection and long-distance haulage of milk by road was begun in the twenties. Though Express Dairies in London had some six-wheeled Sentinel steam waggons (Sentinels always spelt it 'waggons' instead of 'wagons' as with most other makers) they were used mainly in bulk distribution of bottled milk and it was left largely to motor tankers to establish the trunk routes in the milk trade.

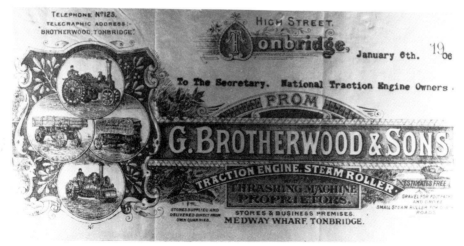

Victorian tradesmen loved ornate letter headings and traction engine owners were no exception to the rule. This is the letter heading used by G. Brotherwood & Sons of Tonbridge. About 1907 the last of the Brotherwood family retired and the business was taken over by Walter Swale, who kept it going for a few more years. It had closed down, however, by 1914

6. The Fair on the Green

It was an epoch-making day for the showmen when, in 1865 Sidney George Soame of Marsham, Norfolk, one of the ingenious race of village engineers, had the notion of driving a roundabout by a small self-contained steam engine built for the purpose and displayed his first example at the village fair at nearby North Aylsham. Until then roundabouts had been powered either by a horse or men walking in a circle or by one or two men turning a handle which drove the ride through bevel gearing.

Soame was a man of modest aspirations and left it to other engineers, more commercially minded, to develop his idea. The most celebrated of these were Frederick Savage of Kings Lynn, Thomas Walker of Tewkesbury and Tidman & Sons of Norwich each of whom established a considerable trade in steam-powered riding machines for showmen adding their own inventions and improvements as the years passed and seeking, whenever possible, to secure for themselves, by patenting their ideas, the benefits accruing from them and making spirited defences of their rights in the courts when patents seemed threatened by a competitor. It was Frederick Savage to whom we must give credit for first building the steam engine into a purpose-built truck of a roundabout – the centre-truck – forming the central pivot of the ride when built-up, thereby enabling the drive to be transmitted by gearing rather than the belt used by Soame.

The advent of steam rides changed the characteristics of the fairs and often caused the actual sites to be varied. The traditional English fair had laid most emphasis upon performances such as boxing, wrestling, juggling, groups of players and acrobats; upon exhibitions, such as camera obscuras, dioramas, peep-shows,

E. H. Bostock standing in front of the Fowler traction engine which caused him so much trouble. The original was a painting owned by Bostock, presumably made from a photograph, and one assumes that the character on the footplate was the ill-chosen 'Greasy Jimmy'

six-legged animals, dwarfs, giants and bearded women; upon games of skill or strength; and upon performing animals. Swing boats, roundabouts and such other riding machines as could be worked by hand or horse power were numerically of relatively little importance. Steam machines altered this emphasis. Not only was it the case that a steam roundabout, merely by the fact that it was steam-driven, attracted a crowd at the expense of other features of the fair, but also that the amount of capital tied up in it made it necessary that it should attract large numbers of riders. Such a machine was, therefore, more suited to large than to small fairs and the rise of steam riding machines led, in the end, to many of the smaller villages losing their fairs altogether.

As the most prosperous and adventurous showmen launched into the purchase of steam machines, often plunging themselves wildly into debt in order to do so, the lesser people of the fairground found themselves more and more on the perimeter of things. David Prince Miller lived the hand-to-mouth life of a fringe showman, wrote – possibly with a slight mishandling of the truth – of his experiences in his *Life of a Showman* and summed it up when he said: 'A fair on the following day, twenty miles distant, funds very low, not more than sufficient to defray the night expenses and no means of getting forward.' The most vulnerable dropped off altogether either into other occupations or pauperdom. Not all the minor showmen gave up, however. Benny Philps (1812–1902), a farmer's son from near Bristol came into fairground life when, as a quick-witted lad fresh from school and handy with his fists, he preferred the rough and tumble of the early nineteenth century fairs to a respectable but stolid life on the farm. His first adventure into ownership was a peep-show and on the strength of his earnings from this he married. Of the two daughters of this marriage the elder, Sally, lost her life in a tragic fire, but Harriet, the second daughter, with a spirit as adventurous as her father's, became his help-mate in his enterprises and, on her mother's death, the keeper of his household. By this time the peep-show had been superseded by a pony roundabout and in the nineties this gave place to an early steam-driven roundabout without platforms. Whilst working on this ride with her father in South London, Harriet met and married William Irvin. My friend Benny Irvin is their grandson. Benny Philps, by that time well into his eighties, seems to have taken a great fancy to his son-in-law and to have treated him as if he were a son. So pleased was he, in fact, that he had the old roundabout relettered 'Philps & Son'. Soon, however, a new set of platform gallopers took the place of the old machine and, for the first time, steam was adopted for haulage in place of horses. Benny died in 1902 leaving William and Harriet as sole proprietors. In 1904, after a short period of difficulty during which both the ride and the engine were re-possessed under the terms of the hire purchase agreement, they bought the set of gallopers still owned and run by Benny Irvin, which had been made eight years before for John Danter, the South Wales showman. To haul it they had another second-hand eight horse power Burrell engine, new in 1892, which William named defiantly 'William the Conquerer'. This ride remained steam-driven and steam-

Double heading a showman's road train up Bunny Hill, Rempstone, Notts. The leading engine is a Burrell and is thought to be the late Pat Collins' 'Empress'. c 1910

hauled until after the 1939–45 war, though in the nineteen twenties it had, however, acquired electric lights in place of the original flares.

Characteristically the fair of the nineteenth century and, for that matter, a good deal of this century was lit by these oil or naphtha flares. One of my earliest memories of a fair is seeing such a flare on a stall go up in flames at Yalding, Kent, probably because of a leaky container, and watching the elderly woman stall-holder beat out the flames, most proficiently, with a sack. It was such a flare that once ran the late 'Jumbo' Wright into trouble at Dagenham one Saturday night. Jumbo's mainstay was an old-fashioned shooter wagon but he had a shellfish stall as a sideline. A leaky naphtha container, hanging from the roof, dripped into a bowl of whelks and, not surprisingly, did little to improve the flavour. Soon he had a crowd of discontented customers milling round the stall shouting that he was trying to poison them. One thing led to another and, doubtless, John Barleycorn lent a hand. The upshot was that they tipped the stall over. The thought of waste was enough to have broken Jumbo's heart. Early next morning he was observed quietly pottering round the site of the mishap picking up the spilt shellfish. Hard though times were on fairgrounds at that time, when fifteen shillings a night was considered good takings on a coconut sheet, Jumbo carried thrift further than most. Once, when he was on an East Anglian fairground, a row developed between a newly married couple in their living wagon. After a bit the crockery began to fly. Presently a plate came out of the window closely followed by a dish of tomatoes. Jumbo hurried to retrieve the fallen fruit. 'Can't waste good wittels,' he said.

To return, however, to the subject of lighting on the fairground and to the old fashioned flare which held sway for so many years, it should perhaps be added that this was not undisputed. Electric light was seen on fairgrounds at least as early as 1890. At first the method of generation was a dynamo mounted on a truck and belt-driven by a portable steam engine but what with the heavy load the engine made for the horses and bother of levelling engine and truck into the same plane so that the driving belt did not run off the pulleys this arrangement soon lost its appeal, though as the late E. H. Bostock, who lit his travelling menageries in this way for a while remarked, 'This (the electric light) was a great feature, quite a number of patrons coming to see it alone.'

Soon Savage and other makers were offering a dynamo and engine combined, on the same truck, under a fixed weatherproof shelter, which improvement eliminated the tiresome levelling and packing but left the anomaly of a powerful steam engine being pulled about the country by horses or sent from town to town by train. Some forward-looking showmen, troubled by the difficulty and expense of horse haulage were already dabbling with steam, either by owning a traction engine themselves or by hiring as required. The logical step, therefore, soon taken, was to place a generator on the traction engine so that it was employed usefully not only when the show was travelling from place to place but also when it was set up. The use of steam haulage by showmen was given a great fillip by the effect of the 1896 Act in liberalising the law relating to the use of traction engines and the improvement of road surfaces together with the spread of steam rolling in this century helped still further.

All the time the use of electricity was confined to lighting, the placing of a generator on every engine did not follow inevitably on the adoption of steam haulage. Electric light was considered by many a luxury that brought no tangible return. The arrival of motion pictures – the early bioscope shows of the fairgrounds – in the closing years of the last century stirred up interest in electricity, however, for gas-lit projectors were inconvenient and sometimes actually dangerous. In this century owners of bioscope shows set the pace in putting generators on to their engines. The owners of the big riding machines were slower to take up electric light but increasingly enthusiastic about steam traction so that by 1910 virtually every major showman was equipped with steam road locomotives. The smaller men were less taken up with steam haulage. A new engine was an expensive item that few of them could afford and many of them carried on, therefore, with their old methods until the big men replaced their first generation of engines with newer and larger examples and second-hand engines came on to the market. For some proprietors of side-stuff, however, a seven or eight horsepower engine, no matter how cheap, was far too big for their needs and for these people a new or second-hand steam tractor or steam wagon provided the answer. Many of them, however, kept going with horses until after the 1914–18 war and made the transition direct from horses to motors.

Going over from horses to a steam engine for transport was not solely a matter of buying the engine. Few showmen, at that time, knew anything about steam and they had to rely, therefore, upon the engine driver they happened to recruit to advise them on its use and to manage the engine. Since fairground life at that time was largely seasonal and synonymous with long hours, rough living and hard work, the men they recruited were often not the pick of the trade. On this point E. H. Bostock may again be quoted. He had replaced his portable engine early in March 1892 by a six-horse power Fowler traction engine and had got through the summer travelling season of 1892 with varying misfortunes, some due to circumstances but many more to the cockiness or ineptitude of his driver. He takes up the story in the late summer:

Eight days later, 11 September 1892, when we were about three miles past New Cumnock on our way south we had another trying time with the traction engine. I may here say that I think I had been very unfortunate in the selection of my engine driver, who was aptly known as 'Greasy Jimmy'.

About three miles out of New Cumnock on the road to Sanquhar there is a long fall into a hollow followed by a steep rise where we always had to assist one another by lending horses from each other's waggons until the lot had been drawn up the hill. As a result of my previous experience of this hill I strongly advised the engine driver to play for safety by taking one waggon at a time, but he pooh-poohed my idea, and of course, I had to bow to his superior

A picture from the camera of the late John Rundle of New Bolingbroke, Lincs, showing the road train of Smith & Warren, the Lincoln showmen. The engine is probably the 8 NHP single crank compound Burrell No 1985 'Mona I'. The first load is the platforms with the trams on top and the second is the centre truck complete with centre pole, laid horizontally on the pole horse. The third and fourth vehicles are packing trucks containing the rounding boards, droppers, top centre shutters, horses, etc; the penultimate vehicle is the organ and the last the living wagon. The date? Probably 1906

knowledge, as I really knew nothing about engines. If my advice had been turned down by a horse driver I should have quickly sent him about his business. Preparatory to the ascent the engine driver halted, stoked up, and had the engine so full of steam that it was issuing from many parts of it. . . . Just as I feared, the engine was not equal to the task of pulling two waggons up the hill, and, of course, it had to stick on the steepest part of the hill. In the circumstances the only thing to be done was to disconnect the back waggon from the front one. This, however, was no easy matter. We had blocks of a good size over which the engine and loads were gradually backing while the driver shouted many instructions which were rendered inaudible by the roar of the escaping steam. I got a very large stone from the side of the road and placed it behind the second waggon. This, along with the other blocks, I deemed would make her secure. You will realise, however, that the engine and front waggon had to ease back a little in order to slacken the connecting pin between the two waggons, and during this operation the second waggon gradually went over the big block. Thus, the moment the pin was released, away down the hill, hind end first, tore the detached waggon.

I stuck to the drawbar for several yards and tried to push her from me in order to deflect the waggon to the side of the road. . . . Just before it reached the foot of the hill where the horses and men were preparing to take up their final load the off hind wheel of the waggon struck the bank. This slewed the waggon right across the road and over on its side. . . .

The engine with half its usual load easily reached the top of the hill and came down to assist in pulling the fallen waggon on to its wheels. . . . It was practically undamaged . . . the animals in the waggon also escaped unhurt.

The showmen were, however, of necessity, quick to learn and by improving their own knowledge soon brought about improvements in their drivers, winning over a better class of man and establishing the nucleus of that corps of seasoned drivers who served fairs up to the end of steam, men like the late Billy Stevens, temperate of speech and sober of judgement, who spent many seasons in the service of the Beachs or the Irvins, or the late Tom Glover, who drove for Thurstons and other East Anglian showmen, the epitome of commonsense and sound experience.

The loads themselves had to be altered to suit steam haulage. Whereas, for horse transport, a set of gallopers might have been spread over as many as eight trucks with steam haulage these could be brought down to four – the centre truck, organ truck, platform truck and horse truck. Nor, with the higher speeds possible with steam and the longer distances between breaks, was it sufficient to have wooden hubs running on a steel or iron axle because of the risk of overheating and the consequent chance of fire. The first improvement was a cast iron bush fitted into the wooden hub but though this was an improvement it was still possible for the bush to work loose and for the wooden hub to rotate about the bush, the resultant friction again setting up overheating and the chance of fire. When on the road such wheels had to be watched carefully for the tell-tale wisp of blue smoke and often the men would be seen trotting alongside the showman's road train to see that all was well with each wheel in turn. There was a good deal of running alongside too to work the hand brakes on the trucks when going downhill. Speeds, on the whole, were not high other than by comparison with horses, particularly if the owner's living wagon was part of the train. Nevertheless some considerable feats were accomplished. The Grays, for instance, are reported to have gone from Hampstead (north London) to King's Lynn, Norfolk in a single day – a distance of about ninety-five miles. Long runs like this could be punishing to wooden wheels even with iron bushes and new packing trucks began to be equipped with one of the various makes of patent wheel, such as the Stagg & Robson or the Tangent in which wooden felloes and spokes and iron tyres were retained but the whole hub was of cast iron. Later still wheels wholly of cast steel began to be used in conjunction with solid tyres, mostly being taken from scrapped heavy steam or motor lorries.

Rubber tyres and better roads took a good deal of the pain out of moving from site to site in the twenties and thirties but the hard work of building up and pulling down the machines at each ground remained. Putting up and taking down a hoop-la or a roll-up was not excessively arduous but the erection and dismantling of a set of three-abreast galloping horses meant heavy work for many hours, carried on whatever the weather. Pulling down had usually to be done overnight, after a day's work. A shut-down at 11 pm and a bite to eat afterwards meant a serious start about half past eleven. The first stage of dismantling a set of Savage gallopers was to unbolt the platform steps, taking care to put every bolt in the right section of the bolt-box. The steps, all of which were numbered, were taken off, in reversed numerical order and stacked. Usually they rode on the platform truck on top of the platforms, and could, therefore, not be loaded until the platforms were on the truck. If removed in reversed numerical order it was easy to pick them up so that after loading they were in numerical order on the truck and, by a reversal of the two events at the destination, to re-erect them in correct order. Incidentally, whilst this was going on others would have taken the foot-step off each horse, carefully replacing the pins.

Next the platform was removed, section by section, the highest number first. The horse rods passed down through the platforms and it was often a puzzle to bystanders how they were removed before the horses were taken down. The answer lay in the flexibility of the structure which hung upon rods from the spinning frame forming the top of the ride. The platform sections rested upon radial bearers – the platform quarterings – which, in turn were hung from the spinning frame by the iron rods. When running this structure was stiffened at its inner edge by jack rods – diagonal rods each running from a hook on a platform quartering to a hook on a swift in the spinning frame and capable of adjustment by a bottle screw at or near its centre. With the jack-rods out it was possible to lift the first platform centre so that its hooks cleared the eyes on the quarterings. The rest of the plat-

A fairground scene of the early twenties, showing equipment owned by Bartletts of Fordingbridge, Hants. The ornate rounding boards of the gallopers can be seen behind the left hand engine (Burrell No 1470). The right hand engine is Burrell No 1909 then newly acquired from J. Studt of Maesteg and still bearing his 'JS' monogram on the motion cover. (*the late A. Arnold*)

form could then be parted enough to allow the loosened platform to be lowered so that it cleared the bottom of the horse rods and could be moved clear of the ride and on to the platform truck. This was hard work and since several of the men doing it were probably casuals recruited for the night's work there might have been a fair number of stubbed toes and nipped fingers with the corresponding amount of bad language.

The horses too were heavy. Each was held up in turn by one of the gaffs whilst the key which held it in the rod was removed. It was then lowered off the rods and removed to the horse truck. The horse rods were then unshipped to ride on hooks on the side of the horse truck. The platform rods and quarterings were dropped off and stowed leaving the ground clear for the organ truck to be pulled clear.

This left the spinning top and the centre to be dealt with. During the early stages of a present day pulling down the light bulbs and the bars that carry them would have been taken down but this would not have been needed in the days when rides were steam driven and lamp-lit. The first step proper in taking off the top was to roll up and stow the canvas tilt forming the roof of the ride. Whilst this was being done one of the engines would have brought the truck alongside which carried the rounding boards – the curved and ornamented fascia around the outer edge of the top. Using the high frame of the truck, usually also the platform truck, it was possible to detach the droppers and rounding boards in sequence rotating the top by hand to get to them in turn, placing each in its own slot in the top of the truck. It was then usual to shunt one of the trucks right under the top and, using it as a working platform, to dismantle the remainder of the top and the top centre shutters, the ornamental panels enclosing the top of the revolving centre.

It now remained to dismantle the pay-box, unbolt the top section of the tall tubular steel centre pole, which, in a steam ride, also doubled as the engine chimney, and lower it by pulleys on to the pole horse which supported it in transit. Lastly the centre truck had to be brought down, on ramps, from the trussed timber 'trams' on which it stood to give it height whilst the ride was built-up. This is done nowadays by a wire rope from a winch on a tractor or lorry. In steam days it was done with an engine using the wire rope and roping drum mounted on the rear axle between the nearside rear wheel and the tender.

This ritual and its obverse of building up had to be gone through every time the machine moved. Two weekends on one site was deemed to be heavenly but two or even three pitches a week not unknown though not many big machines got down to 'day-gaffing' ie opening on a different site each day of the week which many of the little fairs on small village greens had to do – a most gruelling existence. One that did so from time to time was the ornate set of galloping horses

Hauling the centre truck of the Irvin gallopers on to the trams in steam days by means of the wire rope and the winding drum on the rear axle of the engine

owned by the late Alf Bartlett of Fordingbridge, Hants. The famous Hull fair, among major fairs, was, and is, a bad one, however, as showmen had to pull down at Nottingham Goose Fair after Saturday shut-down, move to Hull and build-up in time for opening on Monday afternoon. This meant continuous working, except for any sleep snatched on the loads whilst in transit, from midday on Saturday through to closing time on Monday evening.

Whilst rides were steam-driven and electricity was needed only for lights the engine driver or drivers had an easier time whilst the fair was working. One engine could drive the lights with ease leaving time for washing out the boilers of other engines, doing any adjustments necessary and cleaning. Since the engine, brightly painted and accoutred with twisted brass olivers, stars and rings was such an eye-catcher, each riding master liked to have his engine looking about right but the passion for polish did not stop there. The horses, steps and platforms on a set of gallopers had to be kept clean and, on a wet site, this could mean washing and leathering-off daily. Also the brass casings of the horse rods had to be kept polished, often a job for the children, using a moist cloth and the soft fly ash from the engine smoke box as a gentle abrasive. The living wagon, however, was the vehicle nearest to the heart of the proprietor.

The size of a horse-drawn living wagon was limited by the ability of a team of horses to draw it and all the while horse draught was used wagons remained of modest dimensions. Even then showmen favoured the heavier Burton style of wagon with the body over-topping the rear wheels as opposed to the Reading type with the body between the large rear wheels favoured by the better-off members of the Romany fraternity. Showmen's horse-drawn living wagons tended to be larger and heavier than Romany wagons, often needing two, or even three, horses where the Romany used one. To some extent the differentiation may have been deliberate, for showmen, even in the poverty stricken days of the 1830s, were exclusivists and the *First Report of the Constabulary Commission* (1839) reports, on page 32, that a fairground traveller said his companions were 'merry fellows, money or no money, and laugh at the people for "flats" ' so that then, as now, the showman's term for a non-showman was a 'flattie'. The late George Webb (d 1976), owner of Flanagans Fairs, was a traveller all his life but another traveller once remarked of him, to me, 'Course – he's really a flattie.' He meant, by that, that George's father had been a house dweller before he married Mr Flanagan's daughter and took to travelling. Nor did showmen and Romanies mix and though, as we have seen, members of a showman's family occasionally married 'flatties' it was seldom that the outsider was a Romany. This desire to be different may have influenced the choice of wagon pattern but the latter was soon influenced much more by the advance of steam haulage and by the increasing affluence of the major showmen. In the latter part of the last century those who established themselves as owners of big rides became much richer whilst the smaller men got poorer.

In the late nineties and in this century, therefore, the living wagons of the larger owners took on palatial proportions. Strongly and rigidly built of the best materials, with clerestory roofs for improved lighting and ventilation, they were elaborately panelled internally in mahogany, walnut or bird's eye maple, lavishly provided with brilliant cut and bevelled plate glass in windows and mirrors, carpeted in the best style and provided with built-in furniture and cupboards designed to use every inch of space. Heated, in winter, by coal-burning stoves or even open fires, lit with expensive lamps and ornamented with often magnificent collections of Worcester ware such a living wagon was the source of great pride and material comfort to its owner and his wife and daughters, the latter's appreciation dimmed only by the circumstance that before every move each brittle or fragile item had to be wrapped and stowed to prevent breakage. The side stuff people, however, had to be content with much less, using smaller wagons, perhaps laid aside by the better-off, round-tops, covered carts or even tents. In the inter-war years many found old buses a convenient way of combining living accommodation with transport.

The worst off were the gaff-lads or seasonal hands employed by the showmen, almost invariably flatties. The fair ground was the traditional refuge of men on the run, occasionally from the law itself, sometimes, in the past, from the Army, but often from unemployment, an uncongenial life, a burdensome family or circumstances that had proved too much for the individual. Ernie, for instance, who worked for a couple of seasons for Bennie Irvin on the gallopers, had been a top class chef, until he had suffered a breakdown, and still carried the diplomas he had won. He drifted in one May at Brighton, stayed for two seasons and the winter between and drifted off again, an amiable kindly man with a passion for polish and tidiness. Whilst he was there everything that could be polished *was* polished – the living wagon, the car, the men's trailer, the horses on the ride. Gaff-lads were often fed, or given the chance of being fed, by their employers which, if they were working for the right couple, could mean living very well indeed. Most employers nowadays provide a trailer caravan for their men to live in but in the past they often had to sleep rough in an empty packing truck and wash, if they bothered, in a pail of cold water. On the other hand there were, in steam days, a race of fairground 'steadies', men whom the showmen counted as reliable and who, in turn, worked for the same man or family season after season. Such employees often lived in lodgings or digs. It must be remembered that taking in a lodger was the practice in many village households to supplement, by a few shillings, the weekly budget, A pound a week all found and often, with a kindly landlady, washing and mending thrown in, was the price of tolerable comfort between the wars, and twelve to fourteen shillings (60–70p) pre-1914. Rough lodgings such as were provided at low beer-houses could be had for a few coppers a night, consisting, as a rule, of a bare communal dormitory with a few beds in it, equipped with palliasses and blankets. Such a doss house was run at the 'Star' at Ashford, Kent where, even in the thirties, men paid only six old pence a night.

118

Before 1914 casuals would work all night on pulling down for a couple of shillings (10p) and even between the wars it was possible to get casual labour very cheaply. All hands whether casual or seasonal, in fact received low wages, for the returns of the whole trade were very small. On a big ride the system of fare collection was to have the owner, his wife, a member of the family, or the manager, if the ride was not under direct family supervision, seated in the pay-box. The platform was divided up into sections by section flags, money collection on each section being the responsibility of one of the lads. In slack periods one man could often look after the whole platform but at peak periods four or even six people might have been collecting the money from the riders, each, in turn, paying in at the pay-box. The person in the pay-box would have counted the number of riders on each man's section to see that the cash he turned in was right. As showmen seem, without exception, to have an astounding capability for counting there was little chance of a collector milking his employer's profits by paying in short. If there was any milking to be done, therefore, it had to be the rider who suffered by being short-changed. The practice of gaffs short-changing or 'turning over' (or 'tapping' to use another term) the customers has undoubtedly existed for many years though on some contemporary rides the customer pays direct into the pay-box. From time to time newspapers and periodicals have waxed highly indignant about it but the remedy has always been simple and in the hands of the customer, namely

William Irvin's Foster road locomotive 'Marvellous' soon after the 1914–18 war. Bill Stevens who drove it stands in front of the wheel with his wife and daughter on his right hand, his son – also William – on the wheel above him and an unknown helper on his left. The author has never met anyone who has had a hard word to say of Bill

to tender the right fare, removing at once both the temptation and the means to cheat.

The arrival of a fair in the village was seldom a surprise. The oldest established were generally related, as to date, to some event or time in the year. Thus there were Easter fairs, Whitsun fairs, Christmas fairs, fairs at Michaelmas or harvest, fairs on the first week in this month or the last in that, generally following some ancient tradition, for many village fairs which latterly survived only as pleasure fairs had their roots in commerce; in animal-trading as horse, cattle or sheep fairs, or in the setting up of annual contracts of service for indoor and outdoor servants. One of the most beautifully set of these old village fairs in the south of England is that held during the first week of August at Lindfield, Sussex. Once a sheep fair, it has in the last fifty years or so been held solely for amusement. When I was a boy there might have been six or even seven steam-driven rides and a great number of steam road locomotives, tractors and wagons but now it is all carried on motors. A few days before a fair the ubiquitous fly poster would flit surreptitiously round the village, leaving his handiwork on barn doors, cottage walls, fences and even, to the annoyance of the Post Office, telegraph poles. The posters, printed luridly and, often, crudely, were anything but modest. 'Colossal', 'magnificent' and 'gigantic' were the commonplaces of the epithets, claims to be 'the greatest show on tour' or 'an unrivalled selection' were not rare. Hill Bros of Bristol achieved probably the ultimate in one-up-manship, describing their fairs as 'Hill Bros – the *big* shows'. Except for the most insignificant events fairs were composed of a coming together of many units diversely owned. One of the large showmen secured the ground, unless it was organised directly by municipal owners, and was responsible for the rent of it. He let out plots to the others – his tenants – usually undertaking the bill-posting as part of his responsibilities and equally often taking the opportunity to suggest that the whole outfit was his. Our local showman, Teddy Andrews, of Tunbridge Wells, was more modest than most in this respect, advertising each of his fairs as 'A Large Amalgamated Fun-Fair'.

The great moment of excitement to the village, however, was when the first road train appeared. Children called their friends into the street to see it and to run beside it to the field or the green, drinking in the bright paintwork and brilliant brass of the engine, the elaborate panelling and cut glass of the owner's living wagon, with perhaps a glimpse inside of the 'Hostess' range and its copper kettles, kept from being jarred off the stove by a polished brass rail round the top, the gaudy colours and extravagant claims of the packing trucks proclaiming that the ride packed inside was 'the latest novelty' or 'the sensation of the age' or again, and most improbably, 'patronised by royalty'. All looked bright, exciting and alien. What invested the fair with the romance it exerted is hard to say. Perhaps it was, in part, the sight of a considerable group of people living their lives in caravans, in comfort, cleanliness and some degree of affluence, by contrast with the general squalor of the lives of most of the average run of tinkers and other caravan dwellers seen in a village in those days. Then, again, there was the appeal of the notion of

120

being always on the road and on the move – here today and gone tomorrow – in an age when village life was very static and real holidays a rarity for ordinary people, or perhaps, again, the lure of the air of slight lawlessness associated, usually unjustly, with a fair – the fear that when it moved on the neighbours might be short of some apples from the orchard or a pocket full of eggs from the henhouse or even a few of the hens themselves. As one publican remarked, of fair people in general but really, though he was not aware of it, of the gaff-lads, 'When the travellers come into the bar we even take the cat off the counter.'

Watching the build-up, too, was an excitement – the coaxing of centres into position, the bustle of, to the untutored eye, aimless activity, the shunting in and out of trucks, the lacing of spars and platforms into an intricate structure that, minute by minute grew into an elaborate machine under the fascinated gaze of the onlookers. The culmination, however, was the opening night, exuberant with light, noisy with the shouts of stallholders, the crack of rifle shots and tinkling of broken bottles from the shooter, raucous with mechanical music, in an age starved of ready access to popular music, and pulsing with the steady exhaust beat, softened by the extension chimneys, of the traction engines running light. A day or two more and the whole magic would be gone again, its only traces the trampled grass, a few ashes and the odd fragment of coconut shell.

To some the spell was more than transitory. Arthur Downs was the younger son of an Essex iron-founder, owner of the village foundry at Gestingthorpe in North Essex. The prospect of the fairground held greater allure for him than working for a lifetime in the dirt of a foundry which he knew that, as a younger son, he would not inherit. Except for the period of his military service during the 1914–18 war he spent the remainder of his life on the fairgrounds of East Anglia, much of it with a set of galloping horses. Nor have his sons John and Alan shown any disposition to revert to the static 'flattie' life. John travels a set of steam-driven galloping horses while Alan has a big wheel and a set of chair-o-planes. Even in fairground life Arthur was a nonconformist. When just about every showman had a dog, Arthur preferred a cat and sometimes he had to be pretty brisk in defending his pet against the onslaught of dogs owned by the surrounding showmen.

Dogs, to most showmen, are useful domestic animals, good guards for the wagon and chattels, rather than objects of sentimental regard. Even so they all have names, just as it was unusual for an engine, otherwise esteemed, in an unsentimental way, mainly as an indispensible tool, not to be named. The names bestowed on engines varied from the mundane to the extremely witty. Some sprang obviously from local or national patriotism. Bartlett's 'Pride of the South', Tom Andrews' (father of Teddy Andrews) 'Pride of Kent', John Evans' 'Edinburgh Castle', and Scard's 'King Edward VII' fell into this category along with W. Haggar's 'Cymru am Byth' from Aberdare. Engines were also named after popular heroes or current events. Two successive Burrell engines (No 2354 and No 2355) were named, in 1901, 'Lord Roberts', the first for Henry Thurston in Essex and the second for the Hancocks of Bristol, and in the same way the 1914–18 war produced its 'Kitchener', 'Lord Kitchener', 'Earl Beatty' and 'Sir Douglas Haig'. When, in 1911, 'Uncle' Tom Clarke named his two engines 'King George V' and 'Queen Mary' this, too, followed fairly naturally from a topical event. Nor did one have to look far for origins when Mrs Sally Shepherd of Birmingham called her new engine 'Old Sal'. False modesty did not prevent Mrs Deakin calling the last, and probably the finest, of all Fowler showmens' engines 'Supreme' in 1932. Some engines, again, like 'Queen Elizabeth' and 'Vanguard', were named after famous warships. When Alf Ball of London named his Burrell 'Alfred the Great' there were some base enough to suspect personal aggrandisement in preference to Wessex patriotism. Incidentally, in 1906, when this engine was only a few months old, the driver was unable to control its loads whilst descending East Hill, Dartford and it jack-knifed across the road, fortunately without any personal injury or much damage to the vehicles. President G. H. Kemp, the pioneer bioscope and cinema owner ('President' was his first christian name) made no bones about naming his engine 'President' and a good many other engines were given christian names of members of the owner's family, often of his wife.

Less obvious were the names given to a series of engines bought by G. T. Tuby & Son of Doncaster. 'The Councillor', 'Mayor' and 'Ex-Mayor' marked the progress of the senior partner in the civic affairs of Doncaster whilst his earlier 'St Leger' combined local loyalty with the showman's interest in horse-racing,

The Irvin gallopers, in steam days, fully assembled and ready for the public.

another fruitful source of names. 'Wait and See' was said to have been given its name when the owners, Crowther & Johnson, of Leeds, overheard a chance question 'How on earth are they going to find the money to pay for it?'. When William Irvin, grandfather of my friend Benny Irvin, had his new Foster engine in 1910, his wife wanted it to be called 'Chanticleer' because, after the financial struggles of their early married life, it was thought something to crow about to have been able to order a new engine. William's comment was that it was a marvel that they could afford it and hence 'Marvel' it became, the 'Chanticleer' plate being used to rename the centre engine which had, until then, been known as 'Lily of the Valley', a name given it by John Danter when he owned and used it in the villages of the mining valleys of South Wales. Perhaps the best example of opportunism was the naming of a Burrell tractor 'Russell Baby' after the cause célebre of disputed paternity in the twenties, a name that suddenly became topical for a second time fifty years later when the case cropped up again in the House of Lords in 1976.

Showmen were criticised for being opportunists but when the choice of sites and the selection of pitches on a given site were a free-for-all they had little choice but to seize every opportunity that offered. It was partly to curb the excesses of the intense and sometimes unseemly competition which resulted from this *laissez-faire* situation and in part to band showmen together to resist oppressive actions

A group of relations and friends posed on the gallopers at Wormwood Scrubs in the late twenties. They include George Irvin (on the horse in the centre), his brothers-in-law, Rupert Hewitt (extreme left) and Arthur Traylen (seated centre front) and Arthur's two sons, George and Arthur, bareheaded just behind him

by local authorities which individuals alone did not have the power to fight, that the Showmen's Guild was formed in 1889. Initially known as the United Showmen's and Van Dwellers' Association it changed its name in 1910 when it became clear that other categories of traveller could not, or would not, contribute towards it. By gradually establishing a system of priority of claims by showmen to their established pitches on recognised grounds it helped to eliminate the forced marches and fisticuffs spawned by the old free-for-all system and saved the more vulnerable showmen from the threatened gradual squeezing out by the more powerful characters.

The ability to use one's fists was always admired on fairgrounds, though in more recent years Guild rules have eliminated most of the causes from which fights sprang. Even in the rawer days two or three rounds behind the wagons seldom gave rise to lasting malice and afterwards victor and vanquished often drowned their differences in a couple of pints of beer.

Then, of course, there was the matter of winter quarters. There was not much travelling done between early November and the end of February during which

Building up the ornate set of steam-driven galloping horses owned by Mrs C. Bird in Newbury, Berks, the last fair of the year for many south country showmen. The dating is uncertain but pre-1914. The showman's life of frantic periods of heavy work during building up and pulling down punctuated by placid days when the ride is running took a heavy toll and many widows, of whom Mrs Bird was one, have continued the family business after the death in middle age of their husbands. Even when too old to take an active part in running the ride Mrs Bird used to sit on the steps of her wagon, counting the riders to see that her hired helpers paid in the right money

time travellers 'pulled in' for the winter. Many travelling families belonged to towns and had urban yards into which to retreat in the bad months. Charles Thurston, the Norfolk showman, had a yard, for instance, in Ketts Hill, Norwich; Harry Gray had one in Mitcham, and Harry Hall in Derby. A considerable congregation of showmen used to assemble at the Welsh Harp, Hendon (Middlesex) for the winter. Other families, however, were village folk and kept a field or yard in the home village into which to retreat whilst the fairs were off the road. For instance, Alf Bartlett, owner of the once-famous set of gallopers, made his home at Fordingbridge, Hampshire, Bert Stocks winters in a field at the end of Victory Road, Leiston, Suffolk, whilst John Downs, who travels one of the few remaining sets of steam-driven gallopers, has his winter quarters at Wickham Bishops, Essex. When the longer days and better weather heralded the arrival of a new travelling season, when the engines were unsheeted and steamed up for the first time and the loads drawn out and assembled ready to pull out, it was an exciting day for the village, and there was a steady procession of seekers after jobs. Those attracted to the fair were not drawn solely from the poor or the unfortunate and indeed, many men who worked at threshing in the winter drove or steered a showman's engine in the summer.

The fair on the green provided villagers of the steam era with a valuable, if only occasional, stimulus – either pleasure or annoyance according to temperament – to lives that were otherwise excessively humdrum.

7. The Village Engineers

Nineteenth century village engineers were an ingenious class of men and the tradition of inventiveness and of ingenuity in the use of limited equipment went back to before the days of traction engines or portables. It was, after all, in the mining village of Killingworth, in the Northumberland coalfield, that George Stephenson built his early locomotives, in the teens of the last century, for the colliery railways of the Grand Alliance and in a Cornish village that Trevithick constructed his steam carriage in 1801.

The archetypal ancestor of such establishments was the village forge, a prop of village life and culture which had its roots in prehistoric times. Without question the village metalworker, in every civilisation except, perhaps, our own in the last two decades, has been fundamental to village life – as the maker of implements, utensils and domestic hardware, as co-worker with the millwright and the wheelwright, and as the forger of blades and weapons.

Yet the class of men that we are about to consider in greater detail, who kept the village steam engines in working order, had origins more diverse than direct ancestry from the smith. Some, it is true, could so trace their origins, and the descendents of at least one village smith made the family name famous over large areas of the world. The Garretts had already had a long history as bladesmiths

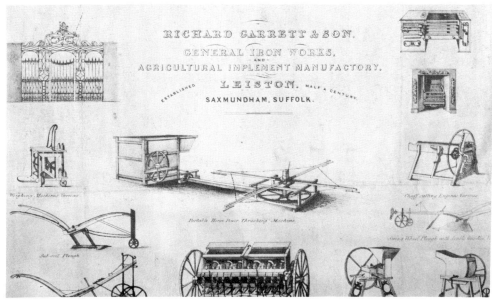

A Garrett poster of c 1828 when the village blacksmith firm was beginning to emerge as an implement manufactory

and gunsmiths in East Suffolk when Richard Garrett, on his majority, took over a forge at Leiston from John Cracey in 1778 in order to continue the family craft. For a generation he continued as a blacksmith employing half a dozen men but when his son, the second Leiston Richard, married Sarah, the daughter of John Balls, patentee of a practical threshing machine, the character of the business began to change. It was their son, Richard III, who really set Leiston Works on the move. By the time he died, in 1866, there were six hundred men on the payroll making fixed, portable and self-propelling steam engines, threshers, seed drills, provender mills, cake crushers, field rollers, tile-making machines, saw benches and general agricultural requisites. The firm made steam engines until 1932 and, as reconstructed in that year, continue as general engineers, within sight of their bi-centenary.

No other village smithy, however, developed in quite a parallel fashion or into quite such a large connection with steam engines. Stanfords of Colchester, where my friend R. C. Stebbing was apprenticed sixty years ago, repaired many of the local traction engines – they had, in fact, from time to time, done repairs on Charles Brown's ploughing engine which blew up – looked after machinery and engines in local factories, repaired agricultural machines and built seed-hulling machines and about one portable engine a year, but twenty-five to thirty men, depending upon the work in hand, was about the limit of their labour force. Colchester, moreover, was a country town, so that Stanfords, important though their position was in relation to village engines, could hardly be considered a village firm.

The yard of Thomas Wood & Sons, Crockenhill, Kent. Under the sheer legs on the right an engine is laid on its side for firebox repairs (*Thomas Wood & Sons*)

J. M. Herridge of Devizes captured this scene on Devizes Green in 1908 when W. E. Chivers & Sons were driving a sewer in headings under it. The three men standing under the tripod of the sheer legs are (left to right) Charles Tilley and Harry Webb (long-standing employees of the Chivers family) and Mr Bellingham, the Borough Surveyor, who directed the work. Behind him (apart from the unknown schoolboy) are Harry Chivers (black jacket) and Bert Chivers (shirtsleeves). The three distant figures in black behind Bert Chivers are (left to right) Arthur Chivers, W. E. Chivers, the founder of the firm, and Cecil Chivers. The steam tractor is a Brown & May, made in Devizes and the road in the foreground so blithely obstructed by the truck is Southbroom Road. (*W. E. Chivers & Sons collection*)

More typical of the purely village works was that of Thomas Wood & Son at Crockenhill near Swanley, Kent. They were the owners of ploughing engines as far back as the eighteen sixties and have owned traction and other steam engines ever since, undertaking in their time threshing, ploughing, road rolling and road haulage. The works that came into being to service these engines included foundries for brass and iron, a smith's shop, a turnery with a lathe big enough to turn the rim of an engine wheel, a paint shop, a carpenter's and pattern maker's shop and a shop for boilersmiths. Though, as far as I know, no new boilers were made there, boiler repairs were undertaken and new rear wheels were made for at least one ploughing engine.

How far replacement parts were home-made, in a well-equipped village works, in preference over purchase from the original makers was a matter of economics. A piece made up at home was generally cheaper than a new part from the makers. Fitting a new part, from either source, involved a good deal of filing, scraping and hand-fitting for each traction engine or roller until almost the final phase – the 1914–18 war and after – was individually fitted together when new without the use of unified machining or fitting limits. Manufacturers, for their part, did not take refuge from their responsibility to supply spares by declaring that the engine for which they were required was of obsolete pattern. As late as 1911 Garretts made and supplied to William O'Neill of Athy, Ireland, spares for a self-moving engine sold to him in the eighteen sixties. The last Garrett road engines to remain in commercial use in Britain were a road locomotive and two steam tractors used by John Harkness & Sons in dock and shipyard work in Belfast which worked well into the 1960s. Garretts kept these supplied with spares until the end. This, admittedly, was exceptional but manufacturer's spares for traction engines remained available, in most cases, at least until the late 1940s. I have cited Garretts not because they were an exception but because the events narrated happen to be within my direct knowledge.

We think of Victorian times as a leisurely age and such, in many respects, they were. The Post Office was, however, incredibly efficient, delivering at least twice daily seven days a week. If a part were found to be broken on a Monday morning and a replacement ordered at once the post could be relied upon to get the letter to the makers the next day. If it was a small part that was required it might be posted back the same night and reach the customer on the Wednesday. Rail deliveries of parcels sent by passenger train were pretty quick also and rivalled the Post Office for speed. By the end of the nineteenth century, with the proliferation of branch lines, few places in England were over ten miles from a railway station which would receive or distribute parcels.

A letter from Mr J. Hollins, a Chepstow haulier, to Manns Patent Steam Cart & Wagon Co in 1910 shows how expeditious the supply of factory spares could be. He wrote, inter alia:

> If anything was worn out or went wrong during the day, when the wagon returned in the evening, I have wired you for parts required and although you are about 200 miles away, I have received them by 6 am next morning, in time to fix them and go on our day's work.

However, though emergencies did happen, most repairs were of a more routine nature or part of a general overhaul and repaint. In such cases if a spare could conveniently be made on the spot or the old part be reconditioned to serve again this was usually done. Boiler making followed somewhat different trends. Setting out and flanging boiler plates was very much a trade of its own and needed, besides, a plate furnace to bring the plates to red heat. In the early days of portable and traction engines boilers were made in which separate pieces of angle iron were used at corners where in later and better practice flanges were formed on the plates themselves. Not much equipment beyond a set of plate rolls was needed to make such primitive boilers using angle iron but as boiler design improved to suit higher working pressures the making of new boilers or even of new fireboxes and tube plates tended to be concentrated in the hands of fewer firms, specialising in boiler work to the exclusion of all else.

Such boiler repairs as new firebox stays, renewal of flue tubes and patching of

Charles Brown's ploughing engine after the explosion at Cressing in 1919

firebox sides, however, were within the scope of most engine repairers, whilst on occasions they fitted new fireboxes or tubeplates made elsewhere, any of which tasks, in the days before power tools and oxyacetylene cutting gear were onerous in the extreme. Drilling out old stays with a ratchet brace meant hour after hour spent in the cramped confines of the firebox pumping away at the lever handle of the drill, and if done in the summer as it often was with a threshing engine, it could be hot and stifling in the box.

Village-built traction engines were less rare in the early days than later but even in this century some of the village firms essayed traction engines of their own manufacture. Of these the most prolific was the firm of C. J. Fyson & Son of Soham, Cambridgeshire who made seventeen traction engines, the first in 1894 and the last in 1924, all of them for use in their own business. The boilers were bought from outside contractors and so were the cylinder castings but otherwise the engines were home-built. Mr R. O. Fyson once said that they undertook the work mainly to provide a useful occupation for their men during slack periods when otherwise they would have had to lay them off.

William Sparrow & Sons of Martock, near Yeovil, Somerset were another firm who built agricultural traction engines at the rate of about one a year. The then head of the firm told me some years ago that the 1914–18 war put an end to the practice but that, until then and since the beginning of the century, they had completed an engine each year in time for the Somerset Agricultural Show at which it was exhibited and sold. Such small scale production was not truly economic but provided an alternative to laying off men when work was scarce though at Sparrows this was, in any case, mitigated by the fact that they were popular repairers with the west of England showmen and often undertook repairs to steam centre engines or showmen's road locomotives during the winter. They had a boiler shop of their own but whether they built all their own boilers neither Mr Sparrow nor Orlando Palmer, who was apprenticed there, could recall with certainty.

Orlando spent over forty years subsequently as a boilersmith in the works of the Eddison Steam Rolling Company at Fordington, Dorchester. A companionable man of inexhaustable cheerfulness and optimism, capable of the direst invective without any real malice, he epitomises the self-reliance and resourcefulness of the men employed in the small engineering establishments, oblivious to personal discomfort and, it sometimes seemed, immune to fatigue. His companion in the boiler shop at Fordington was Bob Forster, a quiet thoughtful man with a good singing voice, a competent flautist and a total contrast in temperament to Orlando to whose extrovert nature his was the perfect complement. Either or both of these two working with the works foreman, the late Percy Balson (1878–1966) on the recovery of a broken-down engine or on clearing up after an accident were a formidable force. It was said that the works was never defeated by a problem of recovery during the whole thirty years or so during which Percy was the foreman.

Fowell No 18 built in 1882 for William Box of Market Lavington, Wilts, the patentee of the design. He used it in his brick and pottery business which was subsequently sold to Holloway Bros, the London builders in whose ownership the engine was when the picture was taken

Among the feats accomplished during those years was the getting up of a big old Fowler compound road roller that had run off the top road at Tyneham near Lulworth and careered down a hundred foot slope, because, it was said, the driver had had too much to drink. He was not too drunk, however, to jump off when she went over. The wreckage was so badly situated that Charles Stewart, Eddison's chief engineer, despaired of recovering it and even a scrap merchant declined it as a gift, asking to be paid to remove the debris. Percy and his men got it up. On another occasion a roller from Newton Abbot depot fell completely through a road bridge into the river below. Again the pessimists wanted to cut it up where it lay but the works team thought otherwise.

Probably the most spectacular recovery of all was that of a roller which had plunged into a gorge at Caponscleugh in Northumberland. Those who knew everything once again shook their heads but with the aid of a pair of Fowler traction engines borrowed from Wear Bros, the sawmillers and hauliers of Hexham, the roller was got back up to the road, patched up enough for it to be towed away and railed back to Fordington works where it was repaired. Percy had friends or well-wishers all over the country. Wear Bros were, to some degree, trade rivals, for they owned and operated rollers. Just the same situation prevailed with B. J. Fry whose works was almost opposite Eddison's. Since both works repaired traction engines they might have been expected to be at loggerheads. Nothing of the sort was the case, however. Percy often dropped in to see B.J. for a chat and if either had a knotty problem on which he wanted a second opinion it was quite likely

A view inside the smith's shop and boiler shop of Cromwell Ironworks, St Ives, Hunts where Fowell traction engines were made

that he would pop across the road for a quick discussion with his nominal rival.

B.J's son, Leslie, was with Percy the day he went to look at the roller at Tyneham. Convalescing after an illness he was invited by Percy to go along in the car for the ride. He was more immediately involved in the clearing up of a mishap at the village of Charminster to the north west of Dorchester. Jack Herbert, the showman, made his winter quarters at the old Flax Mill at Fordington. Just before the incident in question he had engaged some hands for the forthcoming season, one of whom was to steer his Burrell showman's engine 'Majestic', then only seven or eight years old. This steersman must have been a persuasive character for he seemed to have been taken on without the usual practical test of his abilities.

Be that as it may, he steered the Burrell out of the yard successfully, through Fordington, up to the cross-roads by the barracks in Dorchester and down the hill on the Charminster road. At the foot of the hill they bore left on the road to Yeovil. The driver had warned the steersman not to cut in so close to the wall on the hill. Now, on the level across the water meadows, he warned him again to keep the rear wheels well clear of the suspect edge of the road. He was either misunderstood or disobeyed for they were only a few hundred yards further on when the second man cut them in closer than ever and the back wheel went over the edge into the treacherous wet ground. As she went down the driver had time only to shut off steam and grab the side of the cab roof that remained uppermost. The steersman, the cause of the trouble, was not quite so quick on the uptake and was caught by the foot, though otherwise unhurt, as the engine came to rest on its side in the muddy bed of the stream.

Apart from the difficulty of getting the lot out there seemed no great damage and no personal danger. However, getting the steersman's foot free was more difficult than expected. Moreover it soon became evident that the engine was damming the stream and that the water level was rising gradually around the trapped man. At this point it was decided to send for Dorchester fire brigade to pump the water round the engine but when the brigade officer heard where the incident had happened he declined to come as it was outside the borough. Jack Herbert had already fetched B. J. Fry to the scene of the trouble and it took the combined and not unconsiderable eloquence of both and of the police to convince the fire chief that if he did not bring the pump a man would drown. Eventually the pump was sent and the water was pumped from a temporary dam above the engine to another downstream of it. After some digging in the stream bed the trapped man was extricated.

There now remained the problem of the engine and loads. Herbert's Burrell tractor 'St Bernard' was summoned and with it the loads were roped clear and taken back to the yard. B.J. opined that the only way to get the engine out was to obtain several loads of sleepers and jack and pack until a firm base was found and the engine could be levelled up and pulled back up to the road. Another character, however, who had a garage in the town and had had experience at sea, said it could be done by rigging a derrick and lifting the engine with pullies. As this

133

seemed likely to be quicker and, hence, cheaper, Jack Herbert gave him instructions to proceed. Heavy pulley blocks were borrowed hurriedly from the Dockyard at Portland and the poles were rigged. Whether or not the rest of the plan would have worked if a firm footing could have been found for the derrick poles is perhaps questionable. What happened in practice was that as soon as they were placed under load the poles themselves sank into the soil.

Mr Fry's original plan was reverted to, therefore, and the laborious business of jacking and packing in the stream bed was commenced. Eventually a firm bottom was established and finally, after about two days in the water, the engine was up enough for it to be steamed again. 'St Bernard' was scotched up in the road; the wire rope was run out and, with the help of 'Majestic's' own power the latter was hauled up a temporary sleeper ramp and back on to the road. I believe that the big engine was little the worse for its immersion.

In overcoming temporary difficulties the village engineer was adept. Earles of Aldington near Ashford, Kent, were not especially noted for the quality of their fleet of steam traction engines and their methods often left something to be desired, but their men were never open to criticism as lacking in resourcefulness. On one occasion in question they had bought an old engine at an auction, as my informant put it, 'up the shires' – a term of slight disparagement once used a good deal by those fortunate enough to be born in Kent or East Anglia to designate the less fortunate balance of the country. A native might describe an immigrant from these other counties by saying he was 'not a bad bloke but he'd got a touch of the shires in him'. Someone with a touch of the shires had evidently had something to do with this particular engine for when it reached Ashford goods yard by rail, Earles' man who had been sent to fetch it home, found that the bronze screwed plug of the boiler filling opening had been misappropriated. However, this did not deter our hero. Having in his pocket a very good and very sharp pocket knife he cut himself what he deemed to be a suitable piece of hardwood from that which was to hand in the yard, whittled it skilfully to a long and very gradual taper and drove it with the coal hammer into the filler hole. He calculated, rightly as it turned out, that the wood would swell enough to prevent its being forced out by the steam pressure, and his hair-raising makeshift got him home.

George Jarvis, who had a small woodyard in Oxgate Lane, Tenterden, had an old Burrell portable driving a sawbench. Whenever a flue tube had rusted out and leaked he had plugged it at either end, in a similar manner to Earles' driver, by a chestnut plug driven in hard. The plug in the firebox end of the tube charred where it protruded but they remained, so George said, steam and watertight, though the practice would have frightened me. They were still there when he showed me the engine after he had ceased to use it and probably are still, for though the engine was bought subsequently for preservation it has not been retubed at the time of writing.

An engine in which the throttle valve was displaced or broken was sometimes driven home by allowing the steam pressure to fall and then controlling it solely

134

The turnery at Cromwell Ironworks. The large lathe on the right of the picture is for turning traction engine wheels

At one o'clock on a summer Saturday in 1921 or 1922 the late Ted Bannister took this photograph of his workmates leaving off work at the yard of Reeves & Selmes, at Peasemarsh, Sussex. Though the engines are engaged in hauling roadstone they are ordinary Aveling & Porter agricultural engines, a practice which was soon to be abolished by changes in the construction and use regulations relating to road vehicles

on the reversing lever, whilst in at least one case a compound engine in which the high pressure piston had come adrift was coaxed back to the works by dismantling the link motion on the affected cylinder, centreing the valve and taking off the connecting rod. It was then driven as a single cylinder engine on the low pressure side admitting steam through the simpling valve.

The kind of ingenuity that enabled the village engineer to bring home a crippled engine often suggested useful ideas for the improvement of existing methods of construction or use, some of which found their way into patents. Means of improving the springing of engines were a common subject of such patents. George Link of Staplehurst, Kent, designed his own patent spring wheel which Fowlers of Leeds built for him in 1889 whilst William Lambert, of Horsmonden, tackled the problem in another way by inventing his own form of spring axle box with which he rebuilt the Aveling & Porter road locomotive 'Jimmy', owned by him. 'Jimmy' worked for about forty years in its rebuilt form and survives in preservation but no engine manufacturer ever took up the patent axle boxes.

Another proprietor of a village engineering works, Phillip J. Parmiter of Tisbury, Wiltshire invented a light versatile steam tractor in which he kept the ground bearing pressure low by substituting a single wheel, the whole width of the engine, for the customary pair of driving wheels. He also had the idea, reinvented many years later for motor tractors, of putting a transport box on the tractor. Though he exhibited his prototype in 1886 it was not until some eleven years later that he interested a manufacturer in taking it up. As a result of his making the acquaintance of James H. Mann of the firm of Mann & Charlesworth of Leeds, Mann took up the development of Parmiter's patent. Sidney Charlesworth retired from the company shortly afterwards and its name was changed to Mann's Patent Steam Cart & Wagon Co, under which title it built several hundred steam vehicles based on Parmiter's ideas and developments of them.

Wiltshire seems to have been a prolific county for village inventors for it was another engineer from that county, William Box of Market Lavington, who conceived the idea, in 1876, of the Box narrow gauge road locomotive. Concerned at the extra width imposed upon a conventional gear driven traction engine by the inevitable presence of the main drive gear behind one road wheel he designed and built an engine in which the gears drove an intermediate shaft below the boiler, the final drive to the road wheels being by side rods, similar to those on a railway locomotive, thus achieving a reduction of rather more than a foot in the overall width. Four subsequent engines of his design were made by the country firm of C. J. Fowell & Sons of St Ives, Huntingdonshire and two by Robeys of Lincoln. His son, Edward Box, began his steam haulage firm in Liverpool using an engine made in accordance with his father's patent.

Other village firms improved the ancillary equipment of engines. Reeves of Bratton, Wiltshire, Bakers of Compton, Berks and Smiths of Barnard Castle, Co Durham, for instance, produced their own designs of water carts. Thomas Cooper of Great Ryburgh, Norfolk devoted his considerable talents to designing

Part of the lower yard at Horsmonden (Kent) in 1952 showing some of Chris Lambert's 'old gentlemen'. The stocky man wearing the light cap in the middle foreground is the late Bob Cheeseman who served the Lamberts and their successors for sixty-eight years until his death. (*J. H. Meredith*)

a steam digger which could be attached to and powered by a steam traction engine. Cooper diggers really did work and several were sold, but true and lasting commercial success eluded them. It did not, however, elude their inventor, for he became interested in ball bearings when they were first introduced and he was the founder of a considerable firm in King's Lynn devoted to their manufacture.

Wilders of Wallingford, Berks, a country town firm of agricultural engineers nevertheless had the knowledge and the facilities to undertake the rebuilding of an old Fowler single ploughing engine into virtually a new engine, and Goodes of Royston, Herts, tackled the problem of the lack of economy of that same type of engine by conversion to tandem compound ie an engine in which the expansion of the steam takes place in two stages in cylinders of differing diameters, placed one behind the other but having the pistons mounted on the same piston rod. These firms were not large organisations employing extensive staffs of designers and technicians, but country firms headed by men with initiative and inventive powers.

The true province of the village engineer, however, has always been to deal effectively and economically with the problems of repair and renewal brought to him. In the past this often included any kind of machinery from a traction engine to a chaff-cutter, or utensils from a pig trough to a copper kettle. Some of the firms, in addition, earned themselves the confidence of the travelling showmen. It is invidious to attempt comparisons but I have seldom encountered a firm which comes nearer to fulfilling the ideal than that of John H. Rundle of New Boling-broke, Lincs. New Bolingbroke itself is charming. The road through it is raised above the surrounding Fen and has broad grassy margins from which the houses and cottages are set back. The works are on either side of this causeway. On one side is the works house, office, warehouse and foundry, of mainly early nineteenth century origin, and on the other side the more recently built engineering works. For many years it ran, as well as repaired, traction engines; kept the machines of the local farms and estates in good order, maintained fairground rides, made feeding troughs and general ironfoundry and acted as tool merchants and trade ironmongers. There is a heartening and satisfying air about it of continuity and experience – the feeling that if a repair is possible at all Rundles will know how to do it. The business is far from a mere picturesque survival, however, and is an ongoing concern which still remembers and practices parts of the craft all but forgotten elsewhere since the now vanished days when every town or large village had its own foundry.

Often the village foundry led a separate existence but the fact that it was there was a reassurance to the village engineer. Staples of small foundries were firebars and stove bottoms of all kinds, drain gratings, water tanks, feeding troughs and wheel bushes, but many more specialised tasks came their way. Many engine

A village-built traction, the first of seventeen built by C. J. R. Fyson (holding the child behind the engine) at his small works at Soham, Cambs, between 1894 and 1924. He bought the gears of this engine from Fowells of Cromwell Ironworks at nearby St Ives. (*R. G. Pratt collection*)

A works group at Fowell & Son, St Ives, Hunts with Joseph Fowell (arms akimbo) on the right and George Fowell on the extreme left

When Haddenham (Bucks) Baptist Sunday School made an outing to the nearby beauty spot Whiteleaf Cross they travelled behind Mr R. B. Green's Ransomes, Sims & Jefferies traction engine. Tragically, some years later, he was run over and killed by his own engine.

repairers, for instance, liked to cut their own piston rings and would ask the iron-founder to cast the circular iron pots from which they were turned and parted off. A cooperage might order cast iron bung bushes or a millwright plummer-blocks for shafting. Then again it was often a case of 'nip across the foundry and get them to cast a couple of new ones' – which probably meant delivery the next day – whereas now, if welding or brazing does not enable the old part to be repaired it is a case of fabricating a replacement from steel or trying to adapt a standard article. The old-time repairer would have loved welding had it been available to him, however. Joining plates by drilling holes and rivetting or bolting them to-gether was effective but it was hard work. Moreover, the magic spark of the electric welder would often have enabled wear in a component to have been made good where, in the past, the only course was to make or obtain an entirely new part, a point of considerable moment when the plant being worked upon was a large fixed engine with very weighty parts, even allowing for the fact that with their slower running they wore out less rapidly than the present-day equivalent power source.

To illustrate this latter point let me cite the case of the Robey single cylinder horizontal steam engine which drives the brickworks of the Sevenoaks Brick Co at Greatness near Sevenoaks. It has been in its present position for forty-two years, was twenty years old when installed there and has worked on every working day since it was installed. Every day, that is, except the one on which a cylinder cover was broken upon the engine being started before all the condensate water had been drained from the cylinder. Even this cost only two days for repairs. The only other new components needed in that period of forty-two years have been a set of brasses for the bit end and crankshaft bearings. The man who installed it has maintained it throughout those forty-two years. The boiler which supplies the steam is now converted to oil firing and bristles with automatic controls and the plant the engine powers is largely automated but the old engine itself goes reliably on.

In latter years the steam engine was at its best, economically, in situations such as at Greatness brickworks, where the exhaust steam is used to heat a drying floor, or in situations, as in a sawmill, where waste material from the process could be used as fuel. But in the past when the only alternatives were winds or water or, in small applications, the horse the countryside was peopled with steam engines for all kind of uses. Steam pumps were widespread. There were Fen drainage pumps in East Anglia, of which the preserved Stretham Old Engine is a fine example, or pumps built to maintain water in the upper levels of canals, like the great beam engines in the lofty engine house at Crofton on the Kennet and Avon Canal or, again, steam pumps in waterworks. Sometimes these were very modest, like the pumps in the waterworks, which I have already described, at Leigh, the village where I was brought up. Others were larger and intended to pump water to a town. Such were the pair of horizontal Tangyes installed in Hayesden waterworks on the other side of Leigh parish, set up to pump water to the town of Southborough on the hill above. To walk across the fields to Hayesden after church on a summer

Fowell traction engine with outing near East Dereham

Sunday evening, relieve the tedium of the duty engineman by half an hour's chat and to walk home again was a pleasant way of spending the time. The largest and one of the last of these steam pumping stations to be built in the country to serve a town or city was that built by the Metropolitan Water Board in 1929 in the fields of the Thames Valley, near Kempton Park. The engines there, fortunately still working, are quadruple expansions by Worthington Simpson and pump twenty-four million gallons in twenty four hours to serve north and west London. These engines, big enough to propel an ocean liner across the Atlantic, were aloof however, from village life. It was the engine in the mill or brickworks or the estate sawmill that one remembers with most affection – the boiler houses where with luck one could slip in and sit on the form whilst the boilerman rested from firing up or clinkering off and was not averse to talk, and where one might roast a chestnut in the ashes. Such stokers, like many older men of their day, were often great characters. The late Jack Fry, who was one of the firemen to tend the boilers at Curtis & Harvey's powder mills near my old home, was a very large, stout man, amiably lugubrious and a former naval stoker. In hot weather he must have suffered agonies from the heat. Sweat used to pour from him and his party piece was to remove his singlet and wring it out.

The Victorian period which saw the reconstruction of country mansions, particularly those of the parvenu or of foreign potentates, was prolific in introducing fixed or stationery steam engines to the countryside. Indeed when Elveden Hall in the Suffolk breckland was being reconstructed for His Highness Duleep Singh, the Sikh exile who became a Suffolk squire, so much marble and other material was required that a narrow gauge steam railway was laid from Barnham Station on the Great Eastern Railway up to the Hall, though His Highness did

DELIGHTS OF THE PEACEFUL COUNTRY. No. 1.
A Quiet Morning's Ride. A Little Surprise. Meeting the Traction-Engine.

DELIGHTS OF THE PEACEFUL COUNTRY. No. 2.
The Ploughing-Machine.

Punch's view of steam in the countryside

not retain it to handle his household stores in the way that the Duke of Westminster served Eaton Hall by his own 15 inch gauge railway from the Great Western Railway at Balderton Station.

142

Not all reconstructions were on this scale but when Mr W. Astor carried out the restoration of Hever Castle, Kent in 1908 such was the volume of traction engine traffic that he agreed to contribute £2,000 (equivalent to about thirty years' wages for a roadman) towards the reinstatement of the adjoining roads.

Aside from steam haulage by rail or road a major building contract in the countryside might have given employment to a steam crane, steam pile driving frame, steam pump, steam mortar pan or steam concrete mixer. A major civil engineering contract such as the building of the Great Central Railway main line into London in the late nineties or, earlier, the construction of the Manchester Ship Canal during the eighties, was certain to parade before the rural spectators a whole cavalcade of steam-powered construction plant.

Once the fever of construction was past the steam presence was whittled down a great deal but often not banished. Water pumping at wayside railway stations to serve the water column from which the locomotives could draw water gave employment to many pleasant little steam engines. Such a one was installed at the quiet country station at Eridge near Tunbridge Wells, Kent and at Newton Abbott, Devon, pumping was done at one time by hot air engine, an external combustion engine using air instead of steam as the working fluid. From about the nineties progressive owners of mansions, or of large hotels in country areas sometimes adopted the electric light, installing their own steam-driven generating plant. A portable or semi-portable engine belted to a dynamo was frequently a sufficient power source. Parsons, of turbine fame, offered a self-contained set with the whole unit mounted on a frame. When, however, the Great North of Scotland Railway built its palatial Gleneagles Hotel it was completed by its own generating station, equipped, by Willans & Robinson, then a leading firm in the business, with generators driven by compound vertical engines. The demands of the establishment for steam and hot water justified a large boiler installation in any event and it was, therefore, logical to expand the complex to take in a sophisticated – for its time – generating station. So well-equipped was it that it ran well into the 1950s. Such installations were invariably direct current and wherever the owner desired not to generate continuously, as most did not, it was necessary to have a large number of wet cell batteries to store electricity for use during the period when the generating set was not working. As highly inflammable hydrogen gas was given off by the batteries good ventilation and no smoking was the rule in battery rooms.

Except for a few lavish installations like that at Gleneagles these private steam generators mostly gave way, after the 1914–18 war, to motor-driven sets which could be run by a gardener or handyman but in country factories, which needed steam for process purposes, private steam-generating sets ran much longer. Bryants' tanyard at Golden Green near Tonbridge kept up the practice until the last few years and as late as 1944 my neighbour, and former school-fellow, Dennis Goodland, was the engineer responsible for installing a modern, though second-hand, Belliss & Morcom set for them.

It has always seemed entirely logical to me, if low pressure steam is needed for the factory process, that it should be generated at a rather higher pressure and run through a steam engine to power the plant before using the low pressure exhaust for process purposes. This is what was done at the Royal Laundry at Brentwood, part of the group of which my friend, Frank Simpson, was the engineer and his father the principal owner. The engine was a vertical high speed by Allen of Bedford and ran for years with absolutely no trouble, tended by a very competent engineman whose real surname was Roberson but who, because of the then current popularity of the American negro singer and actor, found himself known as Robeson, with the predictable consequence that he acquired the nickname Paul. In a smaller way my maternal grandfather (or, more correctly, step-grandfather) drove the bottle-washing machines in his dairy by steam which subsequently passed through the pipe coils that kept the washing water at working temperature. I remember, in passing, that he was not very pleased one morning when he surprised the boilerman, at a time of heavy demand, with an axe hung on the lever arm of the safety valve. Such double uses of steam no longer prevail here though still practised on the continent and catered for by German boiler and engine makers. In England thrift has become a bore and husbanding of resources equated with meanness or hindered by legislation.

A dying sun lights a dying trade. A view taken in Chris Lambert's yard at Horsmonden on a summer evening in the 1950s

Hundreds of steam engines were scrapped when steam ceased to be commercially important but all were not lost and the public turn out in thousands each week during the summer to traction engine rallies in all parts of Britain. (*B. J. Finch*)

At High Ongar, a village only a mile or two from where I used to stay, the saw-mill of Brace Brothers was run with a Garrett semi-stationary engine mounted over a concrete pit in the boiler house floor, containing a stepped grate which enabled the waste of the mill, sawdust, chips, bark, wane, off-cuts and diseased timber to be fed down into it, even in very large pieces, from floor level. This engine was put in, secondhand, in the nineteen twenties and was still running well in 1975 when it was stopped because neighbours had complained of the smoke.

Certainly village life as a whole is the poorer by the loss of the wealth of steam engines it once had. I cannot imagine that contemporary boys are tempted to linger by windows through which the highly polished and majestic beam of a beam engine might once have been seen in measured motion but which now reveal, if not bricked up against vandals, only a control panel and an electric motor, or to pass slowly by the open doors of engine houses hoping for a word from their hero, the engineman in charge of the mechanical delights within. Such a man was very inadequately rewarded in terms of the world's goods and his modern successor, if he has not been replaced by a computer, is immeasurably better off in all material aspects. What is questionable is whether or not he derives the satisfaction from his work which shaped the engineman of forty years ago into such a fulfilled and estimable individual. It is a question which I leave, unanswered, to my reader.

8. Reflections in Retrospect

Steam engines were part of village life for about a century during what was, probably, a period of turbulent changes in the nation's mode of living. To those of us who have left the half hundred mark behind and who come from village families the steam engine was quite probably the backdrop to our early lives. Its presence certainly affected the lives of our parents or grandparents to an even greater degree.

When, for instance, children of Haddenham, Bucks Baptist Sunday School were to be taken on an outing to nearby Whiteleaf Cross seventy years ago it seemed a very fitting and natural thing to take them in the miller's wagon and two open wagons behind Mr Green's traction engine. The miller's wagon, having a canvas top, was thoughtfully coupled up next to the engine and the cover doubtless kept off the cinders and no-one complained that the journey was slow and the seats hard.

Again whenever an outsize tea boiler was needed for some public jamboree what could be better pressed into service than the village traction engine or portable. How many engines, one wonders, helped their home village to celebrate Queen Victoria's Golden Jubilee or her son's coronation. Nor was the traction engine excluded from family occasions. My late friend Charles Hooker and his bride were taken from the church to the wedding breakfast behind a venerable Aveling & Porter traction engine owned by his father.

Possibly the traction engine made such a deep impression by its being ubiquitous without becoming totally commonplace. This aid in homely tasks and its presence when needed never came to be so taken for granted as are the motor lorry and the tractor today. Nor were engines as transient as motor vehicles. A man might drive one engine for the whole of his working life and live to see his son drive it for twenty years more. Thomas Wood & Son had a ploughing engine built before 1870 which was still working seventy-five years later and even then had several further years of use before it on soil sterilising. Probably the combination of dignity with permanence formed a basis on which the appeal of the traction engine was built.

Notwithstanding the importance of the traction engine to the Victorian agrarian economy and the part it played in heavy haulage for industry there was a large anti-engine lobby, composed of folk of all classes from ostlers and grooms to the noble and patrician, the most vociferous elements of which were drawn from those of the middle classes, often referred to as 'carriage folk', who lived in but did not work in the countryside, being perhaps pensioners of the Armed Forces, retired lawyers or other professional men or simply of independent means.

It is easy to see that their methods of opposition were short-sighted and arbitrary and also that, in the long run, they were ineffective. It is less readily discernible that in part the cause they preached had real weight. It was not, of course, reasonable that they should have expected farms to forgo the use of the steam machines without which they would have had no chance of sustaining the already difficult struggle against the encroachments of cheap imported grain. It was, however, valid to object that, so far as heavy haulage was concerned, neither the steam hauliers nor the industries and cities that benefited directly from their operations contributed to the maintenance or improvement of the rural roads over which their traffic was carried. The first step toward putting this anomaly right was Lloyd George's Road Fund provisions in his 1909 Finance Act. It is possible to sympathise with the objections, prior to that event, of substantial ratepayers in rural areas to being rated for road maintenance necessitated by traffic originating elsewhere and having no relevance to the area in which they lived. Aside from any monetary considerations, however, there is no denying that steam traffic represented an intrusion upon rural peace – with the loss of a silence so widespread and so total as to be unimaginable today – and this, in itself, was a cause of antipathy.

The rise of the motor car diverted and divided opposition to steam traction firstly because motor cars created a nuisance, mainly through dust in summer, that overshadowed both the real or imagined grievances against steam and secondly because, though accusations of neglect had been levelled at steam drivers for allowing their charges to emit smoke, discharge steam or travel too fast, they had never displayed such blatant ineptitude as was now shown by motorists. Commercial rather than legal considerations prevented an untutored driver from being allowed at large with a steam engine but the man who acquired a car was free to drive it as and when he wished, whether competent to do so or not. Road traffic, including steam engines, disarmed much opposition by making a substantial contribution to the war effort between 1914 and 1918 whilst the part played by road transport in breaking the General Strike of 1926 silenced most of the remaining diehards.

Such people, however, were, to most villagers, 'foreigners', not relevant to the continuing flow of life in the village and regarded both by rural employers and employed alike in much the same way as a ship's officers and crew look upon the passengers with whom it is their lot to have temporary contact. Some are liked, some tolerated, some detested and some despised but the ship will go on long after they are all forgotten. Today the structure of village life is different. Farms which once employed twenty men now need only two or three whilst overall village populations have increased. Villages with a common employment for most of the working population, whether in farming, industry or mining, are, therefore, now rare. Populations, too, are more mobile and families smaller so that domination of the population of a village by a single clan or by two or three is rarer. The distinction between the native and the incomer has, therefore, become greatly diminished.

With this change has come about the decline of the village tyrant. Head horsemen on large farms were notoriously jealous of their power and privileges and any of the other horsemen who transgressed the established pecking order did so at their peril. Such little autocracy was not unknown also with the foremen of steam threshing or ploughing sets. Art Jenner, who drove a threshing set for Arnolds of Paddock Wood for years, was a man of most notoriously cantankerous habits from whom it was quite impossible to get a civil answer or comment before the lunch break at 9 am. Some plough foremen were just as bad. A benevolent foreman would give an intelligent cook-boy or an eager third man every chance to learn more about the job. A favoured cook-boy who had brought the foreman his snack would be allowed to stand with him on the engine – where there was plenty of room – to absorb or be instructed in the little practicalities and wrinkles that made a good driver whereas a despot would curse off 'his' engine anyone misguided enough, even with the most helpful and well-intentioned motives, to set foot or lay hand upon it: 'Don't you know your place?'

Even the cantankerous foreman, however, had to placate his farmer clients, however perverse they might appear, for the farmer had the last word. If he did not get what he wanted he gave his work to a competitor next season and no machine owner could afford indefinitely to employ a foreman, no matter how competent technically, who offended his clients. For there is no doubt some farmers were very ready to take offence. For instance there was the man who, no matter how the thresher sieves were set, would complain that the setting was wrong – too much tail corn or too little and corn in the 'seconds' that should have been 'firsts'. Then another would take a handful of corn and complain that the drum was set too close and was bruising the grains and again there would be a grumble that it was too wide and not threshing clean. I am sorry to say that the driver, on whom, in his meal breaks, the burden of adjustments fell would often make a great play, before the farmer, of altering the settings whilst taking care that nothing moved. Judgement was needed in this for there was always the chance that the farmer might know more than the driver attributed to him and recognise the imposition. There would then really be trouble. Drivers, of course, were not all paragons and were not invariably right and nor were farmers always wrong but undoubtedly many complaints were on the principle of 'letting them know who is boss'.

Then there were the bad payers. The giving of long credit was a recognised, if not precisely welcome, feature of trading with farmers, and merchants' credit was a means of finance. Merchants supposedly took into account in their quotations the fact that they were likely to be unofficial bankers and adjusted their charges accordingly. Certainly they were prepared, when tackled, to give a useful discount in return for prompt cash. Asking for and receiving extended credit was one thing but outright evasion of the obligation to pay was another and there were some who, even at the end of an extended period of credit, would temporise and procrastinate about payment. Some used the time-worn expedients to gain time – the misdated or unsigned cheque, or the cheque with a disparity between the sums entered in figures and in writing or even said, 'the cheque's in the post, you should get it in the morning.' Others resorted to counter-claims for damage, usually imaginary, to buildings or machinery. When one contractor would stand no more of it they would go on to the next and lead him a merry dance. Some of these defaulters were, no doubt, devious by nature but in others the manoeuvres were simply manifestations of a desperate endeavour to stay out of the bankruptcy court, and, in retrospect, more deserving of sympathy than censure – not that this helped the threshing contractor to pay his wages, repair bills or insurance.

Until the twenties many agricultural engine owners did not insure at all and fewer deemed it necessary to insure against boiler explosion. Insurance of a boiler through an insurance company meant submitting it to inspection by the company's boiler inspector, a most unwelcome experience to owners who, almost to a man, looked upon their own knowledge and discretion as superior to that of the inspector who, they considered, had the habit of making assurance doubly sure by ordering repairs before, in practice, they were required. The National Traction Engine Owners & Users Association operated a scheme for boiler insurance with underwriters in which the inspection clause was waived in return for a declaration by the owner in the annual proposal form that the boiler was warranted to be in sound working order and free from defects, a warranty which, I consider, took most of the liability off the insurers and made the policy of much diminished value.

Whether because of the way this forced the owners' attention to the condition of the boilers they owned, or because of a more enlightened attitude toward safety at work, boiler accidents on the whole, declined in the last thirty years of steam. Possibly the fact that the use of steam was declining, made the culling out of unfit engines an easier matter, for it is certain that the yards of engine dealers were full of engines, many destined to find no new owners and to end up as scrap. The yard of the late George Taylor of Redbourn, Herts, who doubled up as an engine dealer and scrapper harboured the forlorn carcases of many engines for which hope of finding a new owner had long since perished and which lay there awaiting dismantling. There were, however, firms whose business was to trade in engines as a modern machinery dealer trades in tractors. Such firms were generally repairers and converters of engines as well and sometimes operators in addition. The late E. A. Foley of Bourne, Lincolnshire was a well known dealer in his part of the world whilst, further south Charles Graven at Ely not only dealt in secondhand engines but reconditioned many in addition besides carrying out such tasks as converting military haulage engines into showmen's road locomotives, turning steam tractors into road rollers and converting steam wagons from solid to pneumatic tyres.

Few of the village engineers and engine owners could hold aloof from dealing in engines from time to time. The late Chris Lambert of Horsmonden, whom I have cited before, was an inveterate attender of sales and could rarely resist making a bid for a good engine going cheaply. Whilst steam was still a continuing force he usually sold them again at, one supposes, a profit but toward the end of his life his purchases became more and more motivated by sentiment and his yard was stocked with well-groomed pensioners known in the village as 'Chris Lambert's old gentlemen'. From time to time, Chris, a few of his old drivers and a selection of friends from the Road Locomotive Society would gather at Horsmonden, the engines would be steamed and they would process round the yard or, if licensed and insured, round the village. With his death in 1955 an era of village steam seemed to end. His glance, quizzical but seldom unkind, readily sorted those who knew from those who merely pretended to knowledge which they did not, in fact, possess. To those who sincerely wished to learn he was like a fountain of the unwritten lore of the traction engine. He had taken over the business from his father, a gifted engineer but no business man, rebuilding its fallen finances and keeping it intact through the lean years of the depression by judiciously compounding the functions of steam ploughing and threshing contractor, haulier, engine repairer, sand and ballast merchant, engineer and road contractor; a village jack of all trades, and master unlike the subject of the proverb, of all. Village life is the poorer not only by the loss of its steam engines but of the men like old Chris, with his dry wit and endless empirical knowledge, whose lives did so much for the communities in which they lived.

Appendix: Notes on Leading Makers

Glossaries are tedious and, for this reason, I have tried to avoid the use of technical terms requiring explanation. Some notes on a few of the principal makers whose names appear in the preceding pages may, however, be useful and potted biographies of fifteen leading makes are given below. Six terms recur in these notes – they are:

(i) *Agricultural (or general purpose) engines.* The general run of traction engines, intended for threshing, sawing and other farm or forestry purposes, together with a limited use for road haulage.

(ii) *Road locomotives.* Traction engines intended primarily for heavy haulage having larger bearings, stronger gears and the engine covered by motion plates (to avoid frightening horses).

(iii) *Tractors.* Light road locomotives capable of being managed by one man. First authorised in 1896, one man management was limited to tractors weighing three tons or less but was extended to five tonners in 1903.

(iv) *Rollers.* Essentially traction engines or tractors with broad smooth wheels, the front ones running edge to edge in a fork instead of at opposite ends of the axle.

(v) *Wagons (or 'Waggons' to Sentinel and a few other makers).* Steam vehicles carrying their load upon their own frame as opposed to hauling it. Some had locomotive type boilers, as in a traction engine, but others had vertical boilers (ie boilers in which the central axis of the cylindrical boiler was vertical). Most (but not all) wagons with locomotive boilers were overtypes (ie the engine was on top of the boiler). Vertical boilered wagons mostly had the engine under the chassis ('undertypes').

(vi) *Portables.* Agricultural steam engines on wheels but without means of self-propulsion. Self-moving portables were portables made capable of limited self-propulsion by a chain coupling the engine to a road wheel but lighter, and generally cruder, than an agricultural traction engine.

Notes on leading makers

Aveling & Porter, Rochester, Kent. Thomas Aveling began by making other makers' portables self-moving but in 1860 launched into agricultural engines in partnership with Richard Porter. They made rollers, for which they became world famous, from 1867, road locomotives from c 1871, a certain number of ploughing engines, tractors from 1897, overtype wagons from 1909 to 1925. Failed in 1932 with the AGE combine. They were reconstructed as Aveling-Barford Ltd, at Grantham and continued to sell steam rollers until the 1950s. Now part of British Leyland.

Burrell (Charles Burrell & Sons, Thetford, Norfolk). Began making portables in the late 1840s, followed by self-moving portables and traction engines. Made road locomotives on Boydell patent wheels 1856–1863 and conventional locomotives from 1877. Also some Thomson three-wheeled road steamers. At the beginning of this century they built steam tractors and overtype wagons. Business declined in the twenties and residue transferred to Garretts in 1929. Were celebrated makers of road locomotives for showmen.

Clayton & Shuttleworth, Stamp End Works, Lincoln. One of the earliest commercially successful makers of portables (latter 1840s) for which they became world-renowned. They were relatively slow to take up the traction engine (beginning about 1862). Having evolved a successful design they adhered to it for too long and it was very dated by the nineties when, with Fletcher as their designer, they produced a new and very sound design, followed by a few road locomotives, some rollers, steam tractors and an only moderately successful overtype wagon (in 1912). An undertype wagon was launched in 1920 but was a poor performer. The parent company sank in 1926 but a daughter company (Clayton Wagons Ltd) continued until 1930.

Fodens Ltd, Elworth Works, Sandbach, Cheshire. The business at Elworth began in 1856 but first built a traction engine in 1884, achieving a national fame by a very advanced compound engine shown at Newcastle Royal Show in 1887. The building of tractors and road locomotives was phased out in this century as their overtype steam wagons (launched in 1900) became popular. These highly successful wagons were made until superseded in the early thirties by the diesels which are still made.

Wm Foster & Co, Wellington Foundry, Lincoln. Launched into agricultural engines in the late nineties, following soon with their Wellington steam tractor and a series of 7 and 8 NHP showmen's road locomotives (of which sixty-eight were made during the period 1903–34.) Sixty overtype wagons were made (1919–33). Building of road engines ceased in 1934 but portables were made during the 1939–45 war. The re-named company is still trading. One of the few firms who never made a roller.

J. Fowler & Co (Engineers) Ltd, Steam Plough Works, Leeds. John Fowler began by having his ploughing engines built by other firms but in 1863 set up his own works in Leeds. He was killed in 1864 at the age of 38 but his partners continued and augmented the business. To ploughing engines were added tractions and soon road haulage engines (c 1868). Rollers were made from the nineties onwards and in this century steam tractors. Sales having declined by 1924 they launched a V-engine undertype wagon which achieved only limited success. Steam engine building ceased in the late thirties and the firm was later combined with Marshalls. Fowlers were fine engineers and made a considerable number of showmens' engines as well as some railway engines for both main lines and minor railways.

Richard Garrett & Sons Ltd, Leiston, Suffolk. Beginning in 1778 as bladesmiths, Garretts went on to produce agricultural machines and, in 1848, portable engines. In the next eighty years they produced about 20,000 portables including self-movers. Traction engines were made from 1862–82 and again from 1896–1932. In this century they made rollers, tractors, road locomotives, overtype wagons and (1922–32) undertype wagons. In 1929 the remains of Burrell's business was added to that at Leiston but the failure of the AGE combined (which Garretts had joined in 1919) brought the original firm to an end in 1932. Reconstructed, it is still trading. Garretts were one of the four firms renowned for portables and threshers – the other three were Claytons, Marshalls and Ransomes – which went all over the world.

J. & H. McLaren Ltd, Midland Engine Works, Leeds. The McLaren brothers began to build tractions in 1876 and built their first road locomotive in 1880. Later they built a few rollers and steam tractors but the larger part of their business was in large fixed engines. They specialised in rugged uncomplicated tractions and road locomotives for overseas, built to a high standard. In 1938 they made the last heavy road locomotive of conventional type built anywhere in the world for a South African mine. Fitted with a crane it is now preserved in Johannesburg.

Marshall Sons & Co Ltd, Brittania Works, Gainsborough, Lincs. Marshalls began building traction engines in 1876 with – unusually – an undertype but soon turned to the conventional layout. Besides tractions and portables which were made in great numbers Marshall also made road rollers and steam tractors, threshing machines, fixed steam engines and tea processing plant. Reconstructed after the slump it produced diesel rollers until 1975 when, after a period of decline, the works was taken over by British Leyland. An Indian subsidiary made steam rollers into the early 1950s.

Ransomes, Sims & Jefferies, Orwell Works, Ipswich, Suffolk. Particularly celebrated for their ploughs Ransomes also made threshers and portables from the early 1840s, one of which, as noted in the text, was made self-moving in 1842, but it was not until the 1860s that they took up seriously the making of traction engines. Steam tractors were made in this century but were not important though an overtype wagon, launched in 1920, had limited success. Two showmen's road locomotives were made but generally road locomotives and rollers were left to others. Portables, however, were stocked until the 1950s.

Robey & Co Ltd, Globe Works, Lincoln. Robeys were early in the field with a chain-driven traction in 1859 and built tractions, portables, tractors, a few rollers and road locomotives and steam wagons, mostly overtypes of a design similar to the Ransomes. For many years Robeys made tractions with a narrow front wheel track and short wheelbase for awkward Fen roads. They had a large business in fixed engines for mills and mines.

Ruston & Hornsby Ltd, Sheaf Ironworks, Lincoln. This was an amalgamation of the firms of Richard Hornsby & Sons Ltd of Spittlegate Works, Grantham and of Ruston Procter & Co, Lincoln. The former made an undertype traction engine in 1864 having made earlier portables. Ruston & Procter also made portables and, from the 1870s, traction engines – of an unadventurous design. Hornsbys were pioneers of the oil engine and lost interest in steam quite early but in Lincoln a very fine range of rollers were made and also the 'Lincoln Imp' steam tractor. Oil engine developments displaced steam activities in the late 1920s and continue to this day.

Sentinel Waggon Works Ltd, Shrewsbury. Begun in 1906 as an off shoot of Alley & McLelland of Polmadie, Glasgow the firm was moved to its own works at Shrewsbury in 1917. Although about sixteen overtype waggons (Sentinel insisted on the double 'gg') were made, Sentinel were noted for undertypes which they built for home use and export until the outbreak of war in 1939, the final fling being an order for a hundred waggons for the Argentine in 1950.

W. Tasker & Sons Ltd, Andover. Taskers were blackmiths and implement makers long before their first traction engine appeared in 1869. They built portables, traction engines, rollers and overtype wagons but were never a first eleven firm. They are now chiefly remembered for their 'Little Giant' steam tractors, some gear driven and some chain-driven which were constructed until the 1920s. Being often in low water financially and having been through several reconstructions, now flourishes under its present management.

Wallis & Steevens Ltd, North Hants Ironworks, Basingstoke. Like Taskers they made implements before turning to making traction engines in 1877. They too made portables, rollers, tractors and overtype wagons. Their tractions were simple, reliable and cheap, if not noted for economy of fuel, but their tractors were indifferent and wagons poor. Their 'Advance' rollers, steam or diesel – first launched in the mid-1920s – are among the best rollers ever made and the firm still prospers as a maker of road rollers and road plant and as agricultural machinery merchants. Never in the first rank except for their Advance rollers, but noted for stability and integrity.

There were also a number of traction engine builders of limited output – either because it was subservient to other manufacturers or because the pretensions of the firm were modest. Such firms were, at random: Allchin (Northampton), Savage (King's Lynn), Dodman (King's Lynn), Wantage Engineering Co (Wantage), Fowells (St Ives, Hunts), Humphries (Pershore), Barrows & Stewart (Banbury), Brown & May (Devizes), Davey Paxman & Co (Colchester) and Howards (Bedford). Furthermore there were several firms who made a name, solely or mainly, in steam wagons, notably Thornycroft, Leyland, Yorkshire & Mann, which latter also made a lesser number of traction engines, tractors and rollers. Then, of course, there were very many really small firms, both traction and wagon builders.

Bibliography and Notes for Further Reading

The doyen of writers about traction engines was the late Fred Gillford who ran traction engines at Daybrook, Notts and who wrote about them in his paper *The Traction Engine* published in the Oakwood Press *Locomotion Papers* series in 1952. Another interesting title in that series was Arthur Fay's *Bioscope Shows and their Engines*, written from deep personal knowledge and involvement. I never knew Mr Fay but to talk to Fred Gillford was a revelation.

If I were asked to recommend basic reading on traction engines I would suggest W. J. Hughes' *A Century of Traction Engines* and Ronald H. Clark's *The Development of the English Traction Engine*, in that order. Bill Hughes' book grew from a series of lectures he gave to model engineering societies in the 1940s and 1950s and set out a lucid account of the development of traction engines in Britain. Ronald Clark wrote from a rather different stance, for readers already conversant with traction engine construction and practice, drawing out the way in which individual firms developed their products and grouping his writing under types and periods. His earlier *Steam Engine Builders of Norfolk*, *Steam Engine Builders of Lincolnshire* and *Steam Engine Builders of Suffolk, Essex and Cambridgeshire* were works of more pioneer character setting down the basic facts about the firms who built engines in those counties. *A Century of Traction Engines* and *A History of the English Traction Engine* are, I think, destined to become classics on their subjects.

For those who wish to read more about fairgrounds and their equipment there are three books which are recommended reading – David Braithwaite's *Fairground Architecture*, Eric Cockayne's *The Fairground Organ* and Duncan Dallas's *The Travelling People*. The latter is an account of fairground people, shrewdly observed and reported without cant. *The English Gypsy Caravan* by Ward-Jackson & Harvey, though primarily about the Romanies, gives a fascinating account of the development of living wagons and the history of the firms who made them, which is also applicable to the older generation of wagons used by showmen. David Braithwaite's *Savage of Kings Lynn* is a more specialised account of the Norfolk firm who built many fairground rides as well as traction engines, steam wagons, steam tractors and agricultural machines.

Below is a list of some other contemporary or recent works on the subjects touched on in this book. Mostly these are still in print and where they are out of print they are obtainable through the library system.

Apprenticeship in Steam – J. Hampshire
Burrell Showmen's Road Locomotives – Michael R. Lane
A Century of Traction Engines – W. J. Hughes
Chronicles of a Country Works – Ronald H. Clark
The Compleat Traction Engineman – E. E. Kimbell
The Development of the English Traction Engine – Ronald H. Clark
The Development of the English Steam Wagon – Ronald H. Clark
Discovering Traction Engines – H. Bonnett
Fairground Architecture – D. Braithwaite
A Hundred Years of Road Rolling – Aveling-Barford Ltd
I Worked with Traction Engines – J. Hampshire

My Life in Steam – K. Judkins
The Overtype Steam Road Waggon – M. Kelly
Painted Engines – J. H. Russell
Ploughing by Steam – J. Haining, C. Tyler
Pride of the Road – Michael R. Lane
A Rally of Traction Engines – B. Finch
Ransomes' Steam Engines – A. Beaumont
The Saga of the Steam Plough – H. Bonnett
The Sentinel – W. J. Hughes, J. L. Thomas
Steam Engine Builders of Lincolnshire – Ronald H. Clark
Steam Engine Builders of Norfolk – Ronald H. Clark
Steam Engine Builders of Suffolk, Essex and Cambridgeshire – Ronald H. Clark
Steam Engines at Bressingham – Alan Bloom
Traction Engines – P. Wright
Traction Engines in the North – David Joy
Traction Engines Worth Modelling – W. J. Hughes
The Undertype Steam Road Waggon – M. Kelly
Waterloo Iron Works – L. T. C. Rolt

Index

Page numbers in italic indicate illustrations

Mecchi, J. J., 21, 47
Meikle, Andrew, 16
menageries, 111
Merryweather fire engine, 24
Metropolitan Water Board, 141
Midland Engine Works, Leeds, 152–3
milk collection, 9. 10, 107, *9*
Miles, Charles, Stamford, 90
Miles, Ken, Charmins);er, 10
Miller, David Prince, 109
Milling, 25, 93, 96, *94*
mining, 12–15, *12*, *106*
mole draining, 60, 67, *66*
Motor Car Act (1903), 32
Murch, Umberleigh, 43

naming of fairground engines, 121–3
naphtha flares, 110–11
National Traction Engine Owners & Users Association, 149
Newells, Westerham, 90
newspaper printing, 9
Newstead, Jack, *83*
Nicholls, Rainham 8
Norfolk Motor Transport Co, *103*
North Hants Ironworks, 154

Oliver, George, *86*
Orwell Works, Ipswich, 153
Otterburn, *86*
outings, 146, *139*, *141*
Oxford Steam Plough Co, *79*

Palmer, Orlando, 131
paper mills, 8, 95–6
Parminter, Phillip J., Tisbury, 136
Patten, John, Little Hadham, *65*
Penydaren tramroad, 15
Pethick, Arthur, 74–5, 98
Philps, Benny, 109
Pickfords, 82
Piddle Valley, milk, 9, 10, 107, *9*
Playle Bros, Maldon, *84*
ploughing, 22, 45–65, 66–7, *47–9*, *54*, *58*, *62–3*, *65–6*, *130*, *142*
portable engines, 20–1, 151, *7*, *13*, *19*

Pouts, Whitstable, 64
powder mill, 141
Powell Arthur, 99
Proctor, Frank, Thetford, 47
'Progress', 81
pumping engines, 12–15, 98, 140–1, *12*
Punch, *142*

quarries, 81, 95

Rackham, Reuben, 25
Railways, steam, 8, 15, 18, 104, 107, 141–3
Ramsomes, Sims & Jefferies, 20, 104, 153, *139*
Rastrick, Stourbridge, 16
reclamation, land, 61–2
Reeves, Bratton, 136
Reeves & Selmes, Peasmarsh, *135*
refuse collection, 95, *88*
repairs, 126–45
Rickett, Thomas, 47, *45*
Road Fund, 147
Road locomotives, 10, 20, 74–5, 136, 151, *73*, *77*, *119*
road work, 79–80, 93, 95, *71*, *79*, *80*, *86*, *88*, *93*, *101*, *105*, *135*
Roberts, Glyn Bach, 31, *19*
Robey & Co, Ltd, Lincoln, 9, 33, 74, 97–8, 102–3, 136, 140, 153
Rollers, meaning of, 151
Romaine, Robert, 47
roundabouts, *see* Gallopers
Royal Agricultural Society, 20, 23, 30–1, 50–1, 52–3
Rundle, John H., New Bolingbroke, 138, *112*
Ruston & Hornsby Ltd, 153
Rutherford, Bob, *86*

Samways, Weymouth, 10, *93*
Savage, Frederick, King's Lynn, 108, 111, 114–16, 154
Savory, W. & P. A., Gloucester, 50, 52–3
Sawmilling, 103–4, 140, 145, *3*, *105*
Science Museum, South Kensington, 16

Seaham Harbour Engine Works, 25
Sentinel Wagon Works Ltd, 95–6, 107, 153, *89*, *105*
Sevenoaks Brick Co, 140
Sevenoaks Water Company, 9
Shand Mason fire engine, 24
Sheaf Ironworks, Lincoln, 153
Showmen's Guild, 124
Smithy, Henry, *23*
Smith, William, Little Woolston, 49–50
Smith & Warren, Lincoln, 112
Smithfield Cattle Show, 31, *17*
Smiths, Barnard Castle, 136
Smiths, Lamberhurst, 91, 92
Soame, Sidney George, 108
soil sterilising, 146
South Crofty Mine, *12* *106*
Sparrow, William & Sons, Martock, 130–1
stables, 10
Stamp End Works, Lincoln, 152
Stanfords, Colchester, 127
Staulkey, Tom, *83*
steam, coming of, 12–13, 15–17, 18, 20–2, 29–31, 34, 43ff
Steam Cultivation Development Association (1915), 61
steam, double use of, 144
steam generators, 141
Steam Plough Works, Leeds, 152
steam railways, 8, 15, 18, 104, 107, 141–3
steam rollers, 10, 93, 95, *79*, *80*, *93*
steam tractors, 32, 43–4, 64, 136, 151, *1*, *26–7*, *54*, *57*, *101*, *128*
steam wag(g)ons, 10, 92–3, 95–6, 107, *9*, *10*, *63*, *94*, *96*, *99*, *101*, *103*, *105*
Stebbing, R. G., Earls Colne, 48–9
Stevens, Bill, 113, *119*
Stewart, Charles, 55–6
Stocks, Bert, showman, 125
stone carting, 79–80